Self Publishing Success

Escape the slush pile, automate your indie publishing business and free yourself to follow your writing dream.

Self Publishing Success
The Indie Publishing Machine

Copyright©2019 by Nigel George

All rights reserved. No part of this publication may be reproduced, distributed, or transmitted in any form or by any means, including photocopying, recording, or other electronic or mechanical methods, without the prior written permission of the publisher, except in the case of brief quotations embodied in critical reviews and certain other noncommercial uses permitted by copyright law.

Published by GNW Independent Publishing, Hamilton NSW, Australia

ISBN: 978-0-9946168-8-3 (PRINT)

22 21 20 19   1 2 3 4 5 6 7 8 9

Contents

1—Introduction — 1
- My Journey — 2
- About the Book — 8
- FREE Updates — 11
- Your Own Hero's Journey — 12

2—The Business of Being a Successful Author — 15
- Who You Are — 17
- What is Indie Publishing? — 19

3—The Four Self-publishing Myths — 25
- Myth 1: The Starving Artist — 26
- Myth 2: Indie Books Don't Sell — 34
- Myth 3: Traditional = Real Author — 37
- Myth 4: Traditional Publishers Can Do… — 39
- Traditional Still Has its Place — 44

4—The Five Mindsets — 47
- Mindset 1: There are no Barriers — 48
- Mindset 2: Art and Business are Separate — 49
- Mindset 3: Become an Author Entrepreneur — 51
- Mindset 4: Think Like a Publisher — 53
- Mindset 5: Treat it Like a Business — 56

5—Marketing For Authors — 61
EXERCISE—Conduct a Marketing Reset — 63
The Secret to Successful Book Marketing — 66
Marketing for Authors — 70
The Value Funnel — 76
Your Secret Marketing Weapon: WIBBOW? — 80
Taming the Social Media Beast — 82

6—The Indie Publishing Machine — 87
How it Works — 89

7—Outreach — 95
Outreach is Active — 96
Outreach Content is Sharable — 97
Other People's Lists (OPL) — 98
Being SMART With Outreach — 100
Make Better Marketing Decisions — 104
Prioritize Outreach Activities — 105

8—Create Your Mailing List — 109
Set up MailChimp — 111

9—Author Website Host and Domain Setup — 123
Create a Hosting Account — 127
Configure Your Domain — 134

10—Your Author Website: Set up WordPress — 139
Add Domain — 139

INSTALL WORDPRESS	141
SET UP WORDPRESS	143
ADD PAGES	152
SET UP MENU AND NAVIGATION	157

11—Your Author Website: Content — 165

ADD YOUR BOOKS	165
UPDATE THE ABOUT PAGE	171
ADD POSTS (OUTREACH)	173
CHANGE THE SIDEBAR CONTENT	175
CHANGE THE SITE TEMPLATE	178
ADD MAILCHIMP FORMS	181

12—Publish a Book on Amazon — 195

SET UP KDP ACCOUNT	195
ADD A BOOK	199
ADD A BOOK LINK TO YOUR WEBSITE	212

13—Getting Professional Help — 215

USING UPWORK	217
USING REEDSY	222

14—Outreach FAQ — 229

Q: I'M STILL CONFUSED. IS SOCIAL MEDIA GOOD, OR BAD?	229
Q: WHAT'S THE BEST OUTREACH STRATEGY FOR AUTHORS?	230
WATTPAD	232
SCRIBD	233

Facebook	233
Twitter	234
Instagram and Pinterest	235
Social Automation	235
Author Blog	235
Other Blogs	236
Book Launches	236
Ads	239
Permafree	240
Kindle Select	240

15—Resources — 241

Websites	241
Books	244

Join the Community!

Self Publishing Success is not just a book, it's also an introduction to the indie publishing machine—a site dedicated to providing training and resources for authors wanting to build a successful career.

For lots of free content, tutorials and courses, and book updates, come and join us at:

https://indiepublishingmachine.com

Chapter 1

Introduction

Let me tell you a story about a boy; a boy who wanted to be a writer.

The boy was born into a world where computers were as big as houses, a smartphone was what Max had in his shoe, and social media was Russian TV.

"You can't be a writer," everyone said. "Writers are poor. You need to get a real job."

So the boy did, and he did well at it, but the desire to write never left him. Looking back, he'd spent his career writing—just disguised as computer programs, teaching, writing business manuals, and creating websites for fun and profit.

One day, the boy decided enough was enough. Some might call it a mid-life crisis—the boy preferred to think of it as that point where anyone, regardless of their age, says, "You know what? I'm not putting up with this sh*t anymore."

So, he wrote a book. A terrible book.

Then he wrote another book and sold it to a traditional publisher.

Now, you might think that's the end of the story. A happy ending, indeed!

But it wasn't.

See, in those intervening years, the boy had become a fair corporate manager and entrepreneur, so he knew how business worked. Once the euphoria had worn off, and he had a good look at what he'd signed up for, he realized that this was no dream come true. "I'm getting screwed," he cried. "I can never make a living this way!"

So he wrote another book and sold it to his readers.

Two years later, the boy quit his corporate job and became a full-time writer.

My Journey

I'm sure you've recognized the autobiographical nature of the story of the boy.

I started a voracious reading habit early in life. I decided well before the end of primary school I wanted to create those incredible stories; to one day take readers soaring on flights of my imagination.

Being bookish, fat (back when fat kids were rare) and named Nigel, I guess it was my destiny to haunt the library at school. However, all those years inhabiting the dark corners of the library cemented an already deep obsession with the written word.

By the end of high school, I had published cartoons in the local paper, won school accolades for writing and written a few hundred pages of my magnum opus.

But there was a problem.

It was the late 80s, and I was a math and science kid. For starters, I hated English. I scraped through General English by stringing together bullsh*t with memorized quotes from CliffsNotes. I had no chance of getting an English degree.

The writer's journey was also the road to poverty as those around me were quick to point out. They were right, though—with no real writing skills and no alternative to traditional publishing in a limited local market, my chances of becoming the next Tolkien or King were zero. Zip. Nada.

So, I stuck with the technical track and worked my way up the corporate ladder for 25 years. I started as an electronics technician, then a computer programmer and IT entrepreneur, and spent the last decade in a variety of management roles.

I have nothing to complain about. My work paid well, my partner of 20 years is a wonderful person, and I can get through most days without wanting to strangle either of the boys. But that quiet little voice has always nagged at me.

Well, maybe not so quiet.

My partner, Kate, is intelligent, funny, and tolerant of my many, many faults. Somewhere around the start of 2015, that not-so-quiet little voice must have got the better of her. One night, she looked me in the eye and said, "I love you with all my heart, but this has got to stop. You have a choice—write the damn book or shut the fu*k up and never mention writing again."

Getting such an unambiguous message from the one that matters most in one's life can be an important catalyst. I have never forgotten Kate's message, and it still drives me every day.

So I wrote the book. I sat at my computer early in March 2015 and wrote a 50,000ish word novel in 4 months. Yay!

The problem is, it sucked. Like, total smoldering turd, shall-never-see-the-light-of-day kind of sucked. What made it worse is not long after I finished the draft, I found a folder full of writing from school, and it was worse. I found a short story I was proud of at the time that had a flashback inside a flashback!

Confident I had deluded myself all these years, I decided to write about something I felt I had half a clue—computer software.

Not game enough to try writing a whole book again, lest my non-fiction sucked worse than my fiction, I wrote tutorials for Django, an open source web framework I had enjoyed using in my computer programming days. Don't worry if you have never heard of Django; most non-programmers haven't either.

About ten years ago, the creators of Django published a user manual they later released online for free as an open source book. I decided to update the book to see what feedback I got from readers, rather than take the soul-destroying path of writing a complete book that everyone hated.

That idea worked well. The Django community picked up on the updates and were encouraging in their feedback. So, I kept writing and publishing the updates for free on a website I created.

After a few months, a reader suggested I approach the original publisher of the book to see if they wanted to publish an updated version. I liked the idea, so

I emailed them. The answer was a polite no, but the publisher invited me to chat with an acquisition editor to see if a proposal for another book on Django interested them. After a quick email discussion with the editor, we agreed on a topic of interest, and the editor invited me to submit the proposal.

I expected to never hear from them again, but less than a month later, the publisher emailed me. The senior editor had accepted the proposal, and could I please sign the attached contract.

It's still hard to put in words how I felt when I got that email. I experienced the full range of emotions from black terror to euphoria and back again in the space of a minute. I was a published author. WOOHOO!

Impostor syndrome set in immediately—getting a book deal was an incredible stroke of luck, and I would soon be exposed as a fraud.

I didn't have long to feel sorry for myself, though. Those 20 years of business skills that helped me write a rocking proposal were also about to save my ass when the reality of my tight deadline sunk in.

I would need every time management skill I had ever learned to pull this off. I had 12 weeks to write a book from scratch while working full time in a day job that had nothing to do with computer programming.

To say I was a little crazy in that three months is an understatement. Kate wisely spent about half of it touring Europe with her sister, while our youngest put up with mad dad. But the book got done; by the end of November 2015, it was off my hands and with the publisher.

After finishing the book, I didn't do much with the website until around February 2016, when I tidied up the site and added more content. I was also reading blogs on writing and getting published, and it wasn't long before I dug up material on self-publishing.

Like everyone brought up on the self-publishing equals crap myth, I didn't give it much thought—after all, I was a traditionally published author. Albeit, one who hadn't received more than a small advance for his writing pursuits, but hey, I was on my way.

Meanwhile, I was getting more and more requests to turn the website content into a book. The problem was, the original publisher had declined to update the book, and I knew no other publisher would touch it because of the open source content.

Another writer in the Django community suggested I try *lean publishing*. Lean publishing is where you publish an incomplete book and add content as you go. Traditional publishers in the computer and software space have been doing this for years—they release a book early to generate publicity and revenue for a book before it is complete.

I had a few decent chapters finished and nothing to lose, so I published those first few chapters with the option for readers to pay if they wanted to. It's called Pay What You Want (PWYW). This pricing model is common in indie publishing and is a brilliant idea. You set a minimum price, and the reader can pay any price they want, as long as it's above the minimum. In my case, I set it to zero so the reader could download it for free.

I published the partial book late on 23rd May 2016, turned off my computer and went to bed with my expectations as high as my asking price—zero.

The next morning I checked my emails as usual and got an even greater shock than the publishing offer—hundreds of people had downloaded the book. Some had paid for the book, even though they could download it for free, and I made $21.61 while I slept.

That's a laughably small number, I know, but it triggered a seismic shift in my thinking. People would not only pay for a self-published book they could get for free, but I also received my introduction to the world of passive income—that magical place where you don't have to trade time for dollars.

If you take into account the time invested so far, that 21 bucks equated to around 10 cents an hour, but the book earned $100 in its first week and $1000 in the first two months. For comparison, my traditionally published book paid a $1000 advance it still hasn't earned out.

In the intervening years, the book has returned somewhere between $50 and $60 an hour for the time invested in writing and publishing it—not a bad return on investment at all! I am also grateful the original publisher rejected the offer to update the book. I ran the numbers, and if they had published the book, I would have made a fraction of the money I made as an independent.

It also wasn't a one-hit wonder. I published a third book on Django that made over $1000 in its first week, and over the last couple of years, it has matched the sales of my first self-published book.

In April 2018, my books had made enough money for me to quit my day job.

None of this came easy. I battled through several years of intense learning, false starts, crushing moments of anxiety, frustrations, and fu*kups to get to where I am, and I am still not "there". What I do know, however, is it's possible to make a living from your writing; that the starving artist is just a myth.

And it's not just me. What I did is being duplicated by thousands of other writers around the world—many of whom are doing far better than most mid-list traditionally published authors.

Which brings me to the reason this book exists.

About the Book

The more I research and the more writers I talk to, the more convinced I am that a large number of writers are held back by limiting beliefs. Limiting beliefs, not about their writing ability, but beliefs about the market, publishing, and how to make a living as a writer.

In 2016, I attended a writer's festival in my hometown and went to a panel session with agents and publishers. The panel spent an hour lamenting the decline of the publishing industry and broadcasting how new authors had little chance of escaping the slush pile, and even less chance of making any money.

I could identify the budding authors in the crowd by how much their shoulders slumped during the discussion. I am sure I witnessed the death of many dreams that day.

I was sad for a bit, and then it just pissed me off. It was like an audience of digital photographers taking as gospel the word of a bunch of whining ex-Kodak employees. Why would an author bother listening to these stiffs?

Kindle had been around for over ten years, and many other digital platforms existed. Every author in the audience had global media reach, and I knew indies made half of all author income in all markets. They also made that income at royalty percentages that made 10-20% of net profit look like daylight robbery. Why were these dinosaurs even able to pull an audience?

Not to be harsh on the agents and traditional publishers out there—they do have a place in the modern market, but no longer hold the keys to the kingdom. It's still a valid question, though. Because it was so counter to my experience, I wondered why anyone would let a stranger sh*t on their dreams like that?

So, I did more research and sought an answer to the more succinct "Why would an author consider traditional publishing?"

While I don't believe there is a definitive answer—because we are all different with different goals—there appear to be four broad groups of thinking:

1. Those who subscribe to the myth you are not a "real" author unless you are traditionally pub-

lished. This is the same pretense the literati have shown by ragging on genre fiction writers for decades, even though genre fiction writers make a lot more money than them.

2. Those who write for specific markets where the gatekeepers still exist. For example, imprints that require submissions to come through an agent.

3. Those who over-estimate the difficulty of self-publishing. Self-publishing is not hard, but it does need a consistent business process that must be automated as much as possible so you can concentrate most of your efforts on writing.

4. The budding independent authors that self-published, burned out and convinced themselves that they weren't up to running the business side of their writing. Like group 3, they benefit from understanding the processes that need to be in place for them to become a successful self-publisher.

If you are in group 3 or 4, I wrote this book for you.

I've broken the book up into two parts:

- **Part 1** details what independent publishing is, and addresses the misconceptions authors have about self-publishing.

    It busts the publishing myths that hold you back, outlines the five key mindsets you need to be successful, and shows you how to master book market-

ing such that it doesn't consume your life and your writing time.
- **Part 2** of the book details step by step, how to set up the practical side of your automated, independent publishing business. I show you how to set up your author website, manage your mailing list, publish and market your books, and build your audience through effective outreach.

Or, to put it simply—Part 1 is the inspiration for creating a successful career as an independent author, and Part 2 is the perspiration necessary to set up your automated self-publishing business.

Apart from my own experiences, this book is also the result of a considerable amount of research. Over the last few years, I have read dozens of books, attended about 100 webinars, taken several free and paid courses, and read hundreds of articles and tutorials. Rather than distract the narrative by using in-text references or adding footnotes, I have added a resource list at the back of the book.

FREE Updates

This book is self-published (obviously!). That means I can make changes quickly and easily.

The book publishing market is changing all the time, so I intend to keep the book content updated.

So you don't miss out on changes in the market, I am offering all book purchasers free digital updates. If you bought the paperback on its own, don't worry---as long as you let me know who you are, I will send you a complimentary copy of the eBook when an update is available.

If you find something in the book you don't agree with, is not explained well enough, does not help you, or you think I missed something important, my personal email is nigel@indiepublishingmachine.com.

I suggest, given you will get a free update, letting me know what doesn't work so I can fix it is a far more valuable use of your time (and mine) than trashing the book in a negative review...

You must let me know who you are to receive updates.

Unfortunately, Amazon doesn't let me know who you are, so I can't get the book updates to you unless you join the readers' list.

You can join the readers' list by sending your Amazon proof of purchase to readers@indiepublishingmachine.com.

Your Own Hero's Journey

As writers, we often forget that we are on our own hero's journey. Our paths might be different, with our own trials and tribulations, but we share a common goal: the desire to live our lives as the artist and creator we know we are in our hearts.

It's in the common framework of the hero's journey that there are parallels where we can relate. I, for one, refused the call to adventure for two decades because I thought I had no chance of success.

Have I completed my hero's journey? Not even close. Some days I feel like I'm still floundering in the dark in the whale's belly. Most days, however, I feel like I am facing the challenges of the road, just like every other author.

Think of me as a guide for when you begin your own hero's journey—someone who is a step or two ahead of you, leading you to the right path.

I've learned that building a successful writing career is not as hard as you might think. I've made plenty of mistakes over the last several years; more than I would care to admit most days. I want to pass on the benefits of that experience, to show you how to identify what's important and what's not. Self-publishing success is very much achievable if you understand what's changed in the book publishing world and how to benefit from those changes.

What I hope is that you can accept me as your first mentor—the one that helps you get on your way towards the life you want—the life of a successful author.

You too can slay the dragon.

Chapter 2
The Business of Being a Successful Author

I am lucky enough to have 20-odd years of business experience behind me. My writing is a business, and I have treated it that way since I typed the first word of that rubbish first manuscript.

It's my business background that allowed me to see the advantages indie publishing has over the old traditional publishing business model.

It's my business background that allowed me to filter out the noise, to see past the conflicting and often detrimental advice spouted by various guru's, and dig into the actual data to find what works.

It's these business skills I want to teach you.

My motivation to create this book was to help writers like you see independent publishing for the incredible opportunity it is. I want to show you how to take those first few steps down the road of a career that freed me from a corporate management job in less than three years.

Note I said three years, not three months.

It reminds me of an interview with a sportswoman I watched years ago. The interviewer was touting the sportswoman as the latest overnight success. You could see the interview frustrated her because it took her 12 years of hard graft and sacrifices to become an "overnight" success.

There is nothing overnight about building a successful career as an author. Treating your publishing career as a business also helps to remind you that, like all entrepreneurs, you're in this for the long haul.

In 2018, after I quit the corporate world to write full-time, I was asked to teach self-publishing to a group of authors at my local writers' center. I was more than happy to oblige and created a simple workshop outlining the self-publishing tools and techniques I used to get to where I am.

The feedback from the group was amazing. My students had seen nothing like it before:

- The "gurus" were teaching marketing; I was teaching business fundamentals for authors.
- My students were posting and tweeting themselves into exhaustion; I freed myself from the treadmill with no Instagram, no Pinterest, not a single tweet, and occasional Facebook posts.
- They felt they had no time to write; I wrote and self-published three books while still working full time.
- They were launching to crickets; I launched at #1 in my categories on Amazon.

Without intending to, I had bypassed 99% of the crap online and created a self-publishing model authors believed could work for them.

The only complaint authors in the group had was that there was no time to detail the business principles and the technical how-to of my self-publishing system. What authors needed was a complete resource that helped them set up their own automated self-publishing business to free them to do what they loved—write.

So, I wrote this book—a complete resource that shows you exactly how I put together an automated self-publishing business which also left me with plenty of time to write.

Who You Are

At the highest level, this book is for authors who have worked at their craft and are professional enough to have got relevant and quality feedback. You are the kind of person who knows their stuff is good, but the barriers and bureaucracy of the traditional publishing world frustrate you.

This book is designed to teach you how to build a successful independent publishing business. It is not designed to teach you how to write.

To get the most out of the book, you need to meet most, if not all, of the following criteria:

- You can write a good book, either fiction or non-fiction. There is nothing about the craft of writing in this book. I expect you to have mastered the craft of writing to where you can create a quality manuscript.

- You have at least one book ready for publication or be close. Already published is also good, but if you are traditionally published, you need a book or books where you have full publishing rights.

  If you are close to having a book ready and are struggling to find a good editor, cover design, formatting for print and digital and other services, that's OK. The book contains a chapter on how to find and hire professionals for competitive rates.

- You write books in a genre that sells. It's hard news for some, but it's a truism that a successful book comes in the area where what you like to write overlaps commercial reality. In saying that, anything is possible in modern publishing because you can reach niches traditional publishing has never touched. For example, I came across an article about an author making a good living writing Amish thrillers.

- You want to make money out of your writing. I don't mean a full-time income. While I focus on writing as a career in the book, this may not be what drives you. Making enough to pay down the mortgage faster or take a yearly holiday or spend more on your hobbies may be enough for you. It doesn't matter what your goals are—as long as you have some financial goals. We will talk more about setting goals later in the book.

- I expect you understand there is no "get rich quick." Independent publishing is a business and business is hard—you understand you have to work at it, and often for years, to be successful.
- Finally, you're willing to set aside your preconceived beliefs about what it takes to be a successful author. You may find some ideas in this book a challenge, which is a good thing—change is good! You already know what you have been doing doesn't work; otherwise, you wouldn't be reading this.

What is Indie Publishing?

Before we get started, it helps to define what independent, or indie, publishing is. At the highest level, indie publishing and self-publishing are the same. However, I want you to differentiate in your mind between indie publishing and self-publishing. I want you to think of indie publishing as self-publishing for professionals.

Indies are Professional Self-publishers

Let's face it, self-publishing still gets a fair bit of bad press. While there are examples that justify some of this negativity, much of the bad press now is a last-gasp effort by traditional publishers to prop up their failing business model by disparaging the new reality of publishing.

Sadly, there are also plenty of authors willing to write self-publishing off as the domain of amateurs. None of them will ever read this book though, so you can do what I do and ignore them.

While it is true nothing is stopping Uncle Mike from self-publishing his 600-page memoir about watching paint dry, Uncle Mike is not a professional, and his memoir will disappear along with all the other dross.

I talk a lot about mindsets in this book. What often holds writers back is not a lack of ability, but negative mindsets and assumptions that stop them from making progress. One of these negative mindsets is that self-publishing is a less legitimate way to get your books in front of readers.

So, let's remove the negative baggage and call ourselves independent, or indie, publishers.

We're all professionals here after all.

There is no "Self" in Indie Publishing

There is also a practical aspect to this—there is no "self" in indie publishing. To be successful in your indie publishing business, you will, at some stage, need to hire:

- Editors
- Cover Designers
- Typesetter/eBook designers
- Web Designers

- Marketing Consultants
- An accountant and maybe a lawyer

When you first start, you are likely to do many of these things yourself. As your business grows, however, it's better to outsource these tasks so you can concentrate on your core business, i.e., writing more books. Outsourcing is how small business owners in every industry build their business and is normal.

It's an Online Business

Indie publishing is an online business. While this might seem obvious when you see the high number of eBooks sold each year, most print book sales are also online. In 2017, Amazon alone sold more than half of all print books sold that year.

I don't cover bricks-and-mortar bookstores in this book. While they still make up a substantial part of global book sales, they are irrelevant for a successful indie publishing career.

As long as you put your books into expanded distribution (I will show you how to do this later in the book), independent bookstores will always be able to buy and stock your books.

If you want to get into chain stores or end caps at the airport, you get a traditional publisher to do it for you.

It's Bigger Than Traditional Publishing

Indie publishing is the biggest game in town in terms of units sold. Indies sold 43% of all books sold online in 2017. The so-called Big 5 publishers came in a very distant second with 26% of total unit sales.

Indie publishers come in second to the Big 5 in terms of total revenue; however, indie authors earn more than their traditionally published cousins because of higher royalties.

You Control Your Career

The critical characteristic of indie publishing is that you are in control:

- You choose what type of career you want, what sort of money you want, and how much or how little you promote your work.
- You can write a lot, or you can write a little.
- You choose who gets to see your work and in what format.
- You decide what you're willing to give up and what you expect in return.
- You choose if you want to use a traditional publisher and on what terms.

PART 1

THE NEW REALITY OF PUBLISHING

Chapter 3
The Four Self-publishing Myths

We are in a whole new world of publishing—there has been a fundamental shift in how the business works and how authors make money.

In the past, the only way you could be successful as an author was if you were lucky, rich, or connected. Most times, you needed to be all three.

Now, an author has much more say in the direction of their career. Those who get good at the business of publishing will do much better than their peers, past, and present.

The traditional publishing world is resisting this change, which is understandable. Many authors are also resistant; still willing to accept the constraints and conditions of a broken business model.

With authors though, I believe this resistance is not from an attachment to the old world, but from a set of fundamental misconceptions about what independent publishing is. Many also lack confidence in their ability to take advantage of the new publishing model and build a successful career.

It doesn't take a lot of research to see that there are many myths holding writers back from building a successful career. Out of the multitude of lies and half-truths about writing, I believe four core myths act as artificial barriers to authors being successful.

The four myths are:

1. The Starving Artist
2. Indie Books Don't Sell
3. You Must be Traditionally Published to be a "Real Author"
4. Traditional Publishers Can Do Things You Can't

I often joke I am the Jerry Maguire of nerds. Whenever I hear someone claim the truth of something, I am always saying, "Show me the data!".

It doesn't take much additional research to find data that expose these myths as the pile of nonsense they are.

Building a successful writing career is hard enough, without setting up obstacles in your mind that aren't based on the slightest shred of truth. In this chapter, I will show you research and data that debunks all these myths. I will start with the nastiest of them all—the starving artist myth.

Myth 1: The Starving Artist

If everyone applied their writing craft to this myth, the starving artist meme wouldn't exist. Not only is it both a cliché and a stereotype, but authors need to stamp out its existence with the same diligence as eradicating adverbs and passive voice from their prose.

The starving artist myth leads to a lot of assumptions, the most harmful assumption being that a career as a well-paid author is beyond the reach of all but a lucky few.

The simple fact is there is, and always has been, great gobs of money to be made in books.

In 2017, just under 4.5 billion US dollars' worth of books sold online in the US alone. And this is only online sales—it doesn't include bricks-and-mortar retail sales.

BookMap estimated the global electronic book market to be 122 billion euros in the same year. And that's just eBooks—it doesn't include paperbacks or bricks-and-mortar stores.

It's obvious someone is making money somewhere!

The reason authors have always fed on the scraps of the book publishing gravy train is not that book publishers are a bunch of thieves, but because of the structure of the industry.

Traditional publishing works like this:

1. The bookstore makes a profit selling to the reader
2. The distributor makes a profit selling to the bookstore
3. The publisher makes a profit selling to the distributor
4. The publisher deducts production costs and gives the author 8–15% of what's left.

To illustrate my point, let's try a more concrete example. Let's say you write a mass-market paperback that retails for $14.99.

Paperback Example

Retail Price	**$14.99**
Wholesale Discount	$8.99
Book buyer pays:	$6.00
Less production costs	-$1.50
Publisher gets:	$4.50
You get	**$0.67**
(4% of retail price)	

The book buyer buys the book at the standard wholesale discount (60%)—so they pay $6 for the paperback.

Assuming production costs are $1.50, your publisher gets $4.50.

You get a 15% commission on the $4.50 which adds up to a paltry 67 and a half cents royalty on a book that sells for $14.99—which is about 4% of the retail price.

eBook Example

Retail Price	**$4.99**
Less fees & costs	-$1.99
Publisher gets:	$3.00
You get	**$0.45**
	(9% of retail price)

Your return on an eBook is not much better. If you publish an eBook that retails for $4.99, your publisher will get on average about 60% of the retail price as there are no production costs. Your publisher pays you the same 15% royalty, and you get 45 cents—which is about 9% of retail.

Remember, these are examples to illustrate how the structure of the industry works against you. Looking at royalties from my own traditionally published books, and data from other authors, the numbers err on the side of being generous.

Let's use these numbers to see how they might affect a real author.

If you want to see the starving artist myth in all its glory, you don't need to look past author advocacy organizations. They have all been crying poor for just about forever. Without singling them out, I will use some recent data from the Author's Guild (USA). According to their 2016 members' survey, the median income for all authors was about $8000 a year. We can use this earnings estimate to turn the previous examples into potential sales numbers.

For the sales numbers, I will assume that the author's sales are 70% eBooks and 30% paperbacks (total sales, not total dollars). This is close to the global average on Amazon.

To make $8000, the author needs to make about 12,000 unit sales in a year.

For starters, 12,000 unit sales is great—way more than the oft-quoted, but unverified myth that the average book only sells 500 copies in its lifetime.

The kicker here: guess how much his publisher would make on these sales?

$41,000

Now before you all reach for the pitchforks and knives, am I saying our dear old traditional publisher is pocketing all this money? No.

While some of that money goes towards those plush offices in London, New York, and Paris, most of that money disappears into the massive cost of running a traditional publishing business.

This fact is relevant to the starving artist myth because it's hard to avoid the constant messages of doom and gloom from the publishing industry. You need to see this for what it is—book publishing is not dying. It's going gangbusters as I will show you soon.

Traditional publishers are the ones dying, or at least shrinking at a rapid rate. This contraction of their business model is visible in the many closures and mergers among traditional publishers. It's not book publishing that's failing, but the traditional publishing business model.

For over 100 years, the way to get a product to the consumer was the same:

- The manufacturer supplied goods to the distributor;
- Who supplied goods to the retailers;
- Who sold the goods to consumers like you and me.

When the Internet came along, it enabled manufacturers and distributors to sell directly to the consumer. The Internet had a huge effect on global distribution and retail businesses. These changes are not unique to traditional publishing—the same structural changes occurred in many industries like fashion retail, communications, photography, and electronics.

The new business model looks like this:

1. You make your books available on Amazon;
2. Amazon makes a profit selling to the reader; and
3. You keep the rest.

Amazon is not the only bookseller online, but it is the biggest. The same process applies to Barnes and Noble, iBooks, and others.

Let's see how this new model affects what an author earns. Using the previous examples, for most indie authors, "the rest" is about 60% for paperbacks:

Indie Paperback Example	
Retail Price	$14.99
Less Amazon fees	-6.00
You get	$8.99
(60% of retail price)	

… and 70% for eBooks:

Indie eBook Example

Retail Price	**$4.99**
Less Amazon fees & costs	-$1.60
You get	**$3.39**
	(68% of retail price)

The critical take-home from these numbers is the indie author is making between *7 and 13 times* as much money on each sale as his traditionally published peers.

This folks, is why indies not only hold the keys to the kingdom, but they've run away with the crown jewels too!

So, on 12,000 unit sales, what does this difference add up to for the author?

$72,000

Whoa! Not only is our author far from starving, but they're making more money than the author *and* the publisher combined in the traditional model.

Myth 2: Indie Books Don't Sell

Did you ever hear the story that the average book sells only 500 copies in its lifetime?

Or the one where the average self-published author sells 500 copies and the average traditionally published author sells 5000?

I bet that if you haven't heard the above, you've heard several variations.

So, have you ever stopped to wonder where these numbers come from?

It turns out they come from traditional publishers. For many years, traditional publishers relied on retail book sales statistics that were both out of date and didn't cover the whole book market.

How much do you think we can trust these numbers?

Not at all would be the correct answer.

It's the same answer Hugh Howie came up with a few years back. If you don't know Hugh, he's the guy who wrote Wool and is one of the early Kindle pioneers. He made the first part of his fortune as an indie and megabucks selling Wool and subsequent books to traditional publishers.

It frustrated Hugh that these miserable statistics were the opposite of his own experience and the experience of authors he knew. So, with the help of a data guy named Paul Abbassi, he created Author Earnings—a site dedicated to collecting timely sales data on all books sold on the Internet. Over several years, Author Earnings grew such that it could track millions of book sales in real time.

Unfortunately, Author Earnings shut down in early 2019 so Paul could commercialize the tracking technology. This was a huge disappointment to the thousands of indies who supported him; however, by then, it was too late. The live data was out, and that live data painted a very different picture of the market. So, let's look at what that live data says.

I will focus on eBooks alone to make things simpler. I don't want to bore you to sleep with statistics after all!

Of the US$4.5bn in book sales in the US in 2017, US$1.3bn was in eBooks, with a mind-boggling 266 million individual unit sales.

Indies made up 42.6% of total online unit sales or just over 113 million units. The Big 5 were just under 26% of total unit sales. Which kills the myth dead right there—indies are selling way more units than traditionally published authors. Close to twice as many in fact.

If you take out mega-sellers like Nora Roberts and J.K. Rowling, the numbers are even more skewed in the indies favor. But what about revenue?

In terms of total dollars, indies earned about US$314 million. The Big 5 are still ahead of the indies with US$559 million in overall earnings but remember—this is total dollars earned, not author income.

Total author income has been declining for traditionally published authors since 2015. Most of this decline is because of the Big 5 reinstating agency pricing, or "the great eBook ripoff", where they started charging $10 plus for an eBook. Agency pricing might be good for business, but it hasn't been good for their mid-list authors.

More recent data shows this trend continuing. In a presentation to the Science Fiction and Fantasy Nebula Conference in 2018, Paul showed that the Big 5 still edged out the indies in terms of total dollar sales (41% to 35%). However, the same data showed indies were taking home 3-4 times as much income due to better royalties.

At this stage, I'm sure you've accepted that the indies are making more money, so I assume your next question is: how much money?

This is another easy question to answer with good data.

Analysis of all authors earning more than $50,000 on Amazon alone in 2016 shows that 54% of them are indies—regardless of tenure. The contrast is more dramatic for authors who debuted more recently—80% of all authors earning better than $50,000 a year on Amazon alone are independent authors. This means that the indies are eclipsing the success of their traditionally published colleagues by a factor of 4 to 1.

Yes, $50,000 a year is not rich, but it's a decent enough income for anyone to consider a full-time writing career. Remember, it's Amazon sales income only and doesn't include Kindle Unlimited payouts. For most authors, Amazon is only a part of their total income stream. In my case, it's a little over 50%.

For those of you dreaming bigger, the authors doing a minimum of six-figures on Amazon have very similar proportions. 54% of the long-tenured authors are indies, and 78% of authors who debuted in the last five years and are earning 6-figures on Amazon are indies.

So, not only are indies selling more units, but they're making more money too.

To quote a favorite show of mine: this myth is busted.

Myth 3: Traditional = Real Author

I believe that this is the most insidious myth of all—the assumption that to be a "real" author, you must be traditionally published.

There are two versions of the "traditional is better" myth:

1. Indies don't win literary awards, so traditionally published books must be "better"
2. Anyone can self-publish, but it's tough to get traditionally published, so by definition traditionally published books must be "better"

Version 1 of the myth infects far too many authors, even some of the best. Stephen King has lamented the lack of literary awards in his career, so did Australian author Bryce Courtenay.

It's ludicrous that any writer, famous or otherwise, could value the opinion of a committee, over and above the millions (in King's case, hundreds of millions) of happy readers who have devoured their work over the decades.

As an author who wants to make a career out of your writing, you are an entertainer. Or, with non-fiction, an educator. The measure of your success will always be the number of readers you entertain or educate.

Now, before this ends up sounding like a rant, I understand that as writers, seeking validation is normal. It's why we are forever creating new stories to submit to competitions when we should work on our magnum opus. It's also why we recruit beta readers and reluctant friends and family members to read our work.

So, I get why winning literary awards will always be attractive to writers. However, setting them as the goal of your writing career, rather than a nice bonus for putting out good work is plain silly.

Version 2 of the myth is more dangerous to your career, as it contains a kernel of truth. So, ignoring that traditional publishers also put out a lot of crap: yes, anyone can self-publish. There are no barriers to Uncle Mike publishing his 600-page memoir about drying paint—but this misses the point.

The mountain of dross published each year is no more relevant to your career than the dust bunnies at the back of your bed; they will remain unnoticed until someone cleans them out. The only ones who ever even mention this crap mountain are traditional publishers and misinformed authors who use it as a prop to bash the indie publishing industry.

This myth is why I distinguish between self-publishing and independent publishing. Any fool who thinks they can write can self-publish. However, it takes quality work, a keen eye for detail and strong business acumen to be successful at it.

The belief that the difficulty in getting traditionally published acts as a de facto quality filter is also flawed.

Any editor or agent will tell you that a huge amount of quality work will never make it through the slush pile. Even when a book makes it through the pile, the first question on the publisher's mind is not, "Is this a great book?", it's "Can I sell this?". Publishing constraints also mean that a publisher can still drop a good book because they can't fit it into the schedule.

To cap it off, if your book makes it through, there's a good chance the publisher will pass the book to a freelance editor no more skilled than one you can hire yourself.

Real authors are authors who work hard to improve their craft, put out quality work consistently, and look after their readers. In the modern publishing world, if you nail these three things, you will succeed, regardless of whether you go with a traditional publisher or indie publish your books.

Myth 4: Traditional Publishers Can Do Things You Can't

There was a time, way back in the dark ages, when it was hard to get a book to readers. First, you had to get an agent or a publisher interested in your work. Collecting hundreds of rejection slips was the norm.

Even if you bypassed the system and published your work, you paid thousands of dollars to print a minimum number of copies. Then there was no-one to buy them. Bookstores would rarely stock self-published books, and selling them out of the trunk of your car or at book conventions was hard work.

A very lucky few got through the system and made a success of their writing. Most authors gave up.

Because the publishing world was like this for so long, the myth that traditional publishers can do things you can't still holds writers back today.

Let's break this myth down. The most often cited benefits of a traditional publisher are:

- Traditional publishing has more credibility
- You will get an advance
- A traditional publisher will market for you
- You will get quality editing, covers, etc.; and
- A traditional publisher will get you into bookstores

The first cited benefit is by far the easiest to debunk with a simple question:

"When was the last time you bought a book because you liked the publisher?"

Who published your book is irrelevant to readers. The only person likely to be pretentious about who published your book is a traditionally published author who just learned how much more money than them you earn.

What about advances? While authors often complain about the size of their advances (and how they have diminished over time), nobody has ever complained about getting one. It's a shame because if authors, especially new authors, took a moment to question the status quo, they would see how bad a deal advances can be.

First, there is almost zero chance a new author will get a large advance. There is no hard data available because nobody publishes details, but $5000 is about the maximum from my research.

New authors are susceptible to the advance because they must decide between instant and delayed gratification. New authors often have a nagging question in their mind: *do I take the money now, or do I wait for a better deal?*

Assuming your luck holds and you get a publishing contract, after you receive your advance, you won't see any money in your account for at least a year.

It will take the publisher at least six months to get your book to market. It will then take another six months for you to get royalties because they all pay quarterly, three months in arrears. For example, you will get paid at the end of December for royalties earned in the three months to September.

You will also get nothing in your pocket until you earn out the advance. Before you get your hopes up about that happening, publishers expect that around

75% of the books they publish will never earn out their advance. So in most cases, the "at least a year" I mentioned a moment ago, translates to "never". Depressing stuff!

Using our previous examples, and assuming an advance of $2000, you would only need to sell just over 500 eBooks in that year to equal the advance. The money would also go straight into your pocket the whole time.

There is also the question of rights. A publisher will take as many rights off your hands as they can in the publishing contract. This includes eBook, print, audio, and translations. And you won't get any of those rights back until the book goes out of print, which, given the wording of most publishing contracts, is close to never.

This point is relevant because it's possible the advance is the last dollar you will ever see for the book. There is also no way you can rectify the situation without negotiating a return of the publishing rights to you.

When you self-publish, the rights are yours. Forever.

We can examine the final three benefits—marketing, quality, and coverage—with a simple example. For a new author, a traditional publisher will:

1. Give the book to a professional editor
2. Commission a cover
3. Pass the edited work on to a typesetter/digital layout expert
4. List the book on Amazon (and others)

5. Add the book to distributor catalogs; and
6. Expect the author to do the marketing

If you self-publish your book, you will:

1. Give the book to a professional editor
2. Commission a cover
3. Pass the edited work on to a typesetter/digital layout expert
4. List the book on Amazon (and others)
5. Add the book to distributor catalogs (by checking a box on KDP); and
6. Market your book

Recall our earnings examples from earlier in the chapter? In terms of income, your traditionally published book would need to sell between 7 and 13 times as many copies as your indie published book to equal your indie earnings.

Hmm. You're doing the same work, but have ten times the expectations?

Sorry, but that sounds crazy to me!

There is an obvious "but wait!" here. Can you spot it? Yes, when you publish your work, you will pay for items 1 to 3.

Let's assume you paid $3000 for these services (that's towards the high end). With the huge difference in profit, you would only need to sell 800 eBooks to make all the money back.

The only thing of value that traditional publishers controlled in the past was access to the market. You have always been able to hire editors and cover designers and printers, but without access to the market, you had a high chance of failure.

Now, you can sign up for KDP and make your book available to millions of readers in a half hour. If you publish a quality book that looks professional, the odds tip in your favor. As you saw earlier in the chapter, the data confirms this. Indies are not only selling more units (at least in digital), they're making more money than their traditionally published cousins.

That's it for the four big myths. Before we go on to the next chapter, I want to cover one more thing. Lest someone accuses me of bashing the traditional publishing industry, they do still have a place in modern publishing.

Traditional Still Has its Place

While the point of this book is to make a strong case for indie publishing, that doesn't mean there isn't a place for traditional publishing in the modern market.

My first book is traditionally published, my second sold to a traditional publisher after I self-published it. I sold that book on my terms though—I kept my digital rights and exclusivity on Amazon. I also get paid 50% of net, not 15%.

There's still a place for agents too. They can provide access to markets that require submissions via an agent. They can also provide access to foreign markets where local knowledge is an advantage. For example, I have a recent book with a Korean agent who is shopping around for a buyer for Korean translation rights.

Traditional publishing is still the path to take when you want to take your great-seller and turn it into a mega-seller.

At the top end of town, traditionally published authors still dominate. Examples include long-tenured, mega-sellers like James Patterson, Nora Roberts, George R.R. Martin, and J.K. Rowling. Once you get down to the top 1000 authors, however, more than a quarter of them are indies.

In recent years, the indies have increased their share of this market, and current data shows the rise of Amazon imprints; all of which give the author a better deal than the Big 5.

There is also the 50% of print book sales that aren't online. This is the bookstore market, although these days bookstore is a misnomer—most of these print books sell in department stores and from end caps in airports. Traditional publishing still has a majority stake in this market, although indie-friendly distributors like Ingram Spark and KDP are gaining an increasing share of this space.

Remember though, unless you win the publishing lottery, for your book to be attractive to a traditional publisher, you need to have done most of the work already. Proven success as an indie will also factor in their decision to publish your work. At that point, you must ask yourself whether you still wouldn't be better off on your own.

That's it for the self-publishing myths. I hope I was able to banish any of your misconceptions about self-publishing and opened your mind to the opportunity that awaits you as an indie publisher.

In the rest of Part 1, I'll teach you the practical skills you need to be a successful indie publisher. We'll start with the five mindsets you need to adopt to go from author wannabe to professional indie publisher.

Chapter 4
The Five Mindsets

A successful independent publishing business is not difficult to set up or run; your success has much more to do with your mindset.

You might think that's easy for me to say after being in business for two decades. However, even in junior employees, it's easy to see ultimate success in their chosen career has little to do with ability or circumstance. Their level of success is more often due to how they think about the inevitable challenges they face.

In my experience and the many successful writers I have studied, some common attitudes and ways of approaching the business of indie publishing stand out.

I call these the Five Mindsets. The mindsets are:

1. Successful authors know there are no barriers
2. Successful authors understand art is art and business is business
3. Successful authors are entrepreneurial
4. Successful authors think like a publisher
5. Successful authors treat their writing as a business

Mindset 1: There are no Barriers

Anyone who has a business major will tell you it's a truism that he who controls the means of production has the power. This had been the case since the invention of machines and didn't change until the Internet opened up the world. There is a close parallel between the publishing industry today and the camera industry 20 years ago.

A few big-name companies dominated, with film the only medium used by "real" photographers. Then the digital camera and cheap color printer came along, followed a few years later by the smartphone.

You may argue the finer points of history; however, the takeaway is the means of production (creating and printing a photo) went from being controlled by a few to being available to everyone.

Book publishing is the same. A few large companies no longer control the means of creating a book and getting it to readers. Access to print and digital publishing is available to everyone with an Internet connection.

This doesn't mean becoming a successful author is easy; no more than having a digital camera makes you a photographer. Some will succeed. The majority will fail because they have not learned the lessons I am teaching you. To be a successful author, you don't need a traditional publisher or an agent.

There are no barriers.

Write it down and stick it on your bathroom mirror. Carve it into a plank and nail it to the wall. Tattoo it on your forearm. Whatever you need to do to burn it in your brain because it's the most important mindset of all.

In modern publishing, there is no walled garden, no golden palace. The gates to paradise are an illusion. The path ahead of you leads straight to your success, and there are no obstacles in your way you didn't put there yourself.

I think you get my point. Best to move on before I start to sound like some self-help guru.

Mindset 2: Art and Business are Separate

It's essential for authors to remember when running their indie publishing business that art is art and business is business. Most creatives know this instinctively—Creative Brain is so different from Normal Brain, it's almost like two people are running around in your head.

While this book is about your publishing business, understanding you must make time for your art is a crucial mindset. Without quality products, your publishing business is just a bookshop with empty shelves.

When you are making your art, make art. It's imperative that you develop a mindset that allows you to do your creative work and exclude other distractions. Most authors experience this when trying to keep the editor at bay while in the middle of creating. Separating art and business becomes more difficult for independent authors because they also have other aspects of their publishing business encroaching on their writing time.

Learning to focus by removing distractions is a difficult skill to master, especially in the Internet age where we're besieged by distractions. It is, however, a skill you must learn to build a full-time career as a writer.

Once you "came out" as an aspiring author, I bet it surprised you how many people told you how they always wanted to write a book or had been writing for years.

Ninety-nine out of one-hundred of these people will never publish a book. Not because they all lack talent, but because they will never focus long enough to finish and publish a book.

Even if they do publish one book, they will never achieve the level of long-term focus necessary to publish multiple books and build a profitable career.

I find the best way to develop this mindset is to set aside time in your schedule for creative time.

It can be as little as an hour a day. It can be a day or two a week. Whatever works for you, but that time must be creative time.

Turn off phones and email.

Turn off the Internet.

Ban the family from your workspace.

Be ruthless.

Carving out time for your art can be a challenge to put into practice, so don't be too hard on yourself at first. It's something I still struggle with every week, even after more than a year writing full-time. I work in a home office attached to a house that's empty for 8 hours a day while my wife and son are at work and school, and I still distract myself. However, as I improve at removing distractions, I see my productivity take a step up each time.

My favorite tool for removing distractions is Cold Turkey (https://getcoldturkey.com). Not only is it hard to cheat (this coming from an ex-computer programmer), but it's easy to set up. With Cold Turkey, you set a schedule and a list of programs to block during scheduled hours, and you're done—bye bye Facebook, news websites, HuffPo, Twitter and everything else that distracts you. Cold Turkey will even block gaming platforms like Steam and desktop games.

Mindset 3: Become an Author Entrepreneur

The third mindset is that you must learn to think like an entrepreneur.

The true meaning of entrepreneurship has been butchered by corporate-speak over the last two decades, but the original, and simple definition of an entrepreneur is someone who "… sets up a business and takes risks hoping to make a profit". Setting up the business is simple—it takes only a few hours and requires minimal financial outlay.

For authors, it's the "risk" part that's often the problem. For an introverted author, it's hard to step out of their comfort zone, to take a risk and put themselves out there. However, to be successful as an independent author, you must step out of your comfort zone. You must take on tasks you would rather not do (e.g., marketing and accounting), and you must keep doing them until you win.

Part of becoming an author-entrepreneur is also learning to ask questions that lead to positive action.

An entrepreneur doesn't ask, "Dan Brown's books are full of plot holes and shallow characterizations, why the hell does anyone buy this crap?".

An entrepreneur asks, "Dan Brown can afford to feed Beluga caviar to his cat, how can I emulate his success?".

An entrepreneurial mindset also allows you to see opportunities in the market where others do not. Early Kindle pioneers like Hugh Howey, Amanda Hocking, Joe Konrath, H.P. Mallory and John Locke (to name a few), saw an opportunity in the digital book revolution other authors did not.

While the days of making mega-bucks publishing just about anything are long gone, opportunities still abound if you dare to put yourself out there and take a risk.

It's my firm belief that the unwillingness to adopt an entrepreneurial mindset and take risks is behind so many authors being happy to spend a decade collecting rejection letters from publishers, rather than put out their best work and let readers decide if their work is great or not.

Mindset 4: Think Like a Publisher

For most authors, the next mindset is the hardest to adopt. Once you finish your book, it's no longer your baby, your labor of love, the expression of your heart and soul—it's a widget.

Publishers don't care about a book's artistic use of metaphor, the soaring beauty of Chapter 3, or how the book will make the world a better place. Publishers care about whether the book, among the many books they will publish this year, will sell enough copies to cover the publisher's costs and return a profit.

Publishers don't try to pick best-sellers, because they know it's a fool's game—they wait until a book forges ahead of the crowd and then back it to the hilt. The also-rans are forgotten.

You won't be this ruthless with your work, but it's a helpful perspective for when you finish your masterpiece and put on your publisher's hat.

A finished book is a product, or more accurately an asset. We define an asset as something that generates an income and increases in value over time, like an investment property or shares in a company.

Too many authors think of the Big Win; the one book that will take them from instant noodles in front of the TV to champagne and caviar at the Ritz-Carlton. The problem with this thinking is that you are entrusting your writing career to blind luck. Publishers don't think like this, and neither should you.

You, as a publisher, are a manager of assets. Your books are assets. When you put money into a house or a bunch of shares, you expect to get a return on the investment. With a book, the investment is your time, with some additional costs if you pay for editing, covers, and layout.

So what is a good return on investment you ask?

In investment circles, an average of 7% per annum over time is considered a solid return.

So, if you set your hourly rate to $40 an hour ($80,000 a year), a book that takes 300 hours to produce is an investment of $12,000.

To expand on our simple example, say you invested another $3000 in editing, typesetting and book covers—bringing your total investment to $15,000.

7% of $15,000 is $1050. Can you make $1000 a year? If you were making $1.99 on your eBooks, that's only 40 books a month.

$1000 a year is a much more achievable goal than waiting for a lottery win.

The catch here is you can't live on $1000 a year; you need lots of books earning $1000 a year to make a decent living. If you think of your books as assets, you can see the one-book superstar dream for the con it is.

How many professional property managers do you know own one house? Have you met a wealthy stockbroker who owns one share?

I always tell authors—if you have one book, you have a lottery ticket, but if you have two books, you have the start of an investment portfolio.

You need to stop listening to the "overnight success" stories online. Even in the rare case it's true, you're looking at someone who won the publishing lottery. Your chances of winning are not better than any other lottery.

The immutable math of publishing is where most aspiring indies give up. To make a decent living, you must accumulate more assets (write more books) and get a better return on your existing assets (sell more books).

Lucky for you, this isn't as hard as it looks. It is possible to build a full-time income out of books that don't sell in high volumes by doing it repeatedly. The best thing is, if you keep putting out quality content, each book will increase sales of the rest, so over time your 500 a year seller can become a 5000 or 10,000 a year seller.

Mindset 5: Treat it Like a Business

The final mindset for building an independent publishing career is it is a business, and you must treat it as a business.

Writing a book is just the beginning. Being able to write a book doesn't qualify you to sell your book. Michael E. Gerber (The E-myth) calls this the *Fatal Assumption*—the technical work of a business is not the same as the work required to run a business that does technical work.

Translated to book publishing, this means the craft and skill required to write books is *totally different* to the skills required to sell books.

The primary aim of this book is to teach you the skills needed to run a successful indie publishing business, but it all starts with you developing a business mindset.

Core to adopting a business mindset is to implement the five key criteria for a valid business:

1. A business has business hours
2. A business sets performance targets for employees
3. A business has plans in place
4. A business controls its finances; and
5. A business hires experts

If you are missing any of these key criteria, you don't have a business; you have a hobby.

A business has business hours

Even if business hours translates to "after the kids go to bed", you need to allocate that time and be ruthless in protecting it.

You wouldn't keep a job long if you watched TV or went to the pub instead of turning up to work. You must treat your publishing business with the same level of respect.

A business sets performance targets for employees

A business expects a certain level of performance out of its employees.

You need to set production targets for yourself. In its simplest form, this is a word quota. A more comprehensive approach could be a project plan for your next book—complete with a deadline and significant milestones.

A business has plans in place

A business needs a plan.

The plan does not have to be a complicated, written document, but you do need to have a firm grasp of the basics:

- How many sales do you need to make each month to meet your income goals?
- If your sales are not achieving your goal, how do you plan to fix it?
- What rights do you want to manage yourself and what rights would you like to license to others? Rights include digital, audio, print, regional distribution, and translations.
- When a traditional publisher comes knocking at your door (and they will), what would you be willing to license to them and on what terms?
- Agents will also approach you in time. An agent is unnecessary in most English language markets. They can, however, be useful for getting you into publishers that use agents as gatekeepers, or for foreign markets that need local expertise. You must plan for this eventuality, so you don't give away the farm in your excitement.

A business controls its finances

You must be in control of your finances.

As a minimum, you need a spreadsheet to record your publishing income and expenses.

You should also register your publishing business as a proper business. The rules vary from country to country, so I can't provide any specific advice, but when you are running a business enterprise, most countries allow you to claim legitimate expenses. A serious business person takes advantage of all the benefits their country's laws provide.

A business hires experts

Hire professionals where you can.

Remember, there is no "self" in indie publishing. You are running a small business and will need professional help for tasks where you lack the skills (or the motivation). I appreciate this can be tough early on, as we often start with little money. However, as I will show you in Chapter 11, you can find professional help for many publishing business tasks, even if you're on a tight budget.

That's it for the five mindsets. In the next chapter, we will cover the one thing all authors struggle with — book marketing.

Chapter 5
Marketing For Authors

In this chapter, we will tackle the biggest perceived barrier to publishing success—marketing your books. In the surveys I have done, and in the research data I have looked at, writers are often confused about how to market their books, or frustrated with poor returns despite spending more time marketing than writing.

Of all the bad advice a budding writer can find online, marketing advice is by far the worst. In one ten-minute search, it's possible to find several examples of so-called "marketing secrets" regurgitated ad nauseam; many of which flat out contradict each other.

This cancer doesn't just infect book marketing, but it has a greater impact on writers because if you are wasting time following this advice, you're not writing. As I wrote earlier, the immutable math of book publishing is to increase your success, you must write more and sell more.

I am sure because of all this bad advice going around, many of you are approaching this chapter with some trepidation. You needn't worry—while some of the following might be difficult to accept because it's contrary to what you have heard, my approach to book marketing is dead easy to implement.

As you will see, in book marketing, less is more.

Don't believe me?

Well, here are some of my own stats:

- I have two social media accounts—Facebook and LinkedIn. I have never created an account on any of the other platforms
- I do nothing with my LinkedIn account except update my profile once in a blue moon
- I infrequently post on Facebook
- I have never paid a cent for advertising

Today's big name authors were around before social media existed. J.K. Rowling wrote the whole Harry Potter series before having a Facebook account and even the darling of the indies, Hugh Howie, was well on his way when Facebook had less than 100 million users and MySpace was still a thing.

I am not singling social media out here, but this is where 99% of online marketing advice is directed. As I will show you in this chapter, social media can be useful, but it's no panacea.

Before we move on, I am not saying all marketing advice is terrible, but a sensible business person questions its source. Always remember that most online marketing gurus make their money selling you their "secret formula", not from using the formula. This is the good old-fashioned "selling the sizzle" tactic used by the multi-level marketing industry for decades.

EXERCISE—Conduct a Marketing Reset

NOTE: This exercise is for authors who have been marketing their books. If you don't have a book ready or have not marketed your books yet, you can skip to the next section.

I want you to stop for a few minutes and complete an exercise for me. Don't skip this because I bet once you have completed the exercise, you'll feel a million bucks.

We're going to conduct a marketing reset.

Chances are, you have tried several things to spread the word about your books and increase sales. Chances are also that most of them didn't work, or you aren't sure if they worked.

This exercise eliminates everything that doesn't work for you, so you can concentrate on the things that do.

Step 1

Write out everything you have done in the last 12 months to promote your books and increase sales. It doesn't matter what order, we'll get to that next.

Step 2

Cross out everything on the list that didn't result in an increase in sales. It doesn't matter if you're not sure at the moment—go with your gut feeling on what worked and what didn't.

With some of these activities, you will question yourself; you will wonder whether something you did caused them to fail. Don't do this—go with your experience, not on what some guru says should or shouldn't have worked. If you don't think it worked for you, cross it off.

Step 3

Look at the items you haven't crossed out yet. Your list should only include items you are confident increased sales.

For each remaining item, ask yourself, "Was it worth the effort?"

This is an important step, so take your time.

Consider the time and money you spent on the activity. Looking at the results, would you do it again?

In Part 2 of the book, I will show you how to calculate the return from a marketing activity, but let's leave the math for now and go with your gut feeling again—anything you don't think was worth the effort, cross it off the list.

Step 4

Reorder the remaining activities (assuming you didn't cross everything off the list), so the most beneficial is at the top of the list, and the least beneficial is at the bottom of the list. You can go with your gut feeling again if you're not sure. Don't worry if this is all guesswork at the moment, I will show you in a later chapter how to collect accurate data.

If you crossed everything out, that's OK.

Step 5

Stop doing everything you crossed out. Right now.

Never do them again unless you learn something new and want to try them again.

How do you feel?

Like a huge load has been lifted?

Like you might find time to write now?

I hope so. I know when I sat down and worked out what was working and what wasn't, my business changed forever. I was doing less work and making more money. In fact, for six months in 2017, I was so busy at the day job, I did nothing at all—not a single social post or update or email—and my monthly income didn't drop in any noticeable way.

So, now you have completed the exercise, you should have a short list of things you know help your writing career. Your list may be empty, but that's OK too because I am about to show you what works.

The Secret to Successful Book Marketing

Book marketing is the most misunderstood part of the independent publishing process. It's the most common reason why authors don't self-publish or have been unsuccessful at self-publishing. How many times have you heard (or said yourself!):

- "I hate selling"
- "It's too complicated"
- "I will never get time to write"
- "I posted until my fingers bled and only 3 people like me"

These statements are common because it's easy in our modern, information-overloaded society to lose the signal in the noise. And it is noise, especially for authors—because the underlying signal, the one fundamental tone that makes it all work, is so simple most authors kick themselves for not realizing it sooner.

There is only one proven marketing tool for authors, and it's one you already possess.

It's your writing.

This doesn't mean you publish your book and hope for the best—this is "build it, and they will come" thinking, and we know that doesn't work. To go from zero to an independent author making a good living, you must first overcome one barrier. This barrier isn't money or your lack of industry contacts, it's not geography, and it's not your lack of 3 million fans on Facebook.

It's trust.

When you think about it, it's obvious—what do we value above all things online? It's trust. We go to the sites we trust the most; we only buy things from sites that have the padlock and trust logos. We are wary when a stranger contacts us. It's the reason why we ask our friends for recommendations, read reviews, check out a book's star ratings, and read the sample chapters.

When a potential new reader comes across your work, trust is the only barrier, and the trust question is simple:

"Will I enjoy reading what this author has to say?"

If the answer is a confident yes, they will buy your book. Simple as that. This is the same for fiction or non-fiction, except with non-fiction the reader is looking to learn something rather than for entertainment.

And when they've finished your book, if they like it, they are not only more likely to read your other books, but they will also recommend it to their friends.

This is why your writing is the single most powerful tool in your marketing toolkit because giving a potential reader the opportunity to read your work allows them to make a definite decision whether they like your work enough to buy your books.

It also explains why blogging and all forms of social media are lousy places to sell books because there is no way any of these forums can provide as definitive an answer to the trust question than reading your work.

Which brings us to the chicken and egg question: "How will they know if they like my work enough to buy it when they need to buy it to see if they like my work?"

The answer is simple:

You have to give it away. For free.

And not the meh stuff, your best stuff.

This is counter-intuitive, ridiculous even, and terrifying. Most authors resist giving their work away, but it is critical to you having any long-term success.

Internet marketers don't often agree on anything, and each guru is convinced they hold the recipe to the secret sauce, but do you know the one thing they all agree on?

Growth only happens when you create content that users want to share.

And free stuff is infinitely shareable, as it provides potential readers a zero-risk way of sampling your work. Unlike cat videos and celebrity memes, readers place a high value on you sharing your creative talent, and they will reward you with their trust and loyalty.

This fundamental principle underpins all discussions of platform, ninja marketing, 6-figure launches, and whatever else is the flavor of the month. When you understand this, most of the stress and confusion related to book marketing disappears.

Understanding you must give stuff away to grow your career is key to your success. It's what took me from picking up scraps at the fringes to making enough money to quit my corporate day job. And it wasn't a simple cheat sheet or two I gave away: I published a 650-page textbook that took me 14 months to write in its entirety on my website for free.

This principle is what honest educators in the indie space will teach you. When you research successful indies, you will find all of them are giving great content away. A perfect example of this principle in action is Andy Weir, author of *The Martian*. He published *The Martian* in parts on his website until his readers demanded he turn it into a book so they could buy it. And they did—in their thousands—and as you know, the rest is history.

There is a wrong way and a right way to do this, which I will show you in Part 2. The super-important takeaway from this chapter is that success as an author, indie or otherwise, has nothing to do with how many social media followers you have. What matters is putting out high-quality content, and gaining the trust of readers by providing them with a zero-risk way to sample your work.

Now you understand the secret behind becoming a successful author, I will explain my simple and effective approach to marketing for authors.

Marketing for Authors

Once you realize the secret to book marketing is building trust with potential readers, you can see there is nothing sleazy or even difficult about book marketing.

You do not "sell" books, nor are you trying to make people buy your book—you are putting it out in the market and making it easier to find for those who are already looking for a book just like yours. In fact, if you are chasing sales, you're doing it wrong.

Of course, the devil is always in the detail—first, you must filter out all the readers who will never be interested in your work, so you can concentrate on engaging those that will. This is easier said than done, given most of the published marketing advice is flat out wrong for authors or has a very poor return on time invested.

To better understand the process of successful book marketing, I will use a staple of all marketing textbooks—the marketing funnel. Many of you may have seen variations of this concept, but they all mean the same thing: we pass through six stages before we buy something.

You can apply these stages to a book purchase:

1. **Awareness**. The reader is aware they can buy a book online.
2. **Interest**. The reader would like to buy a book to read.
3. **Consideration**. Do they want to read a thriller or a sci-fi?
4. **Intent**. The reader decides they want to buy a thriller, so they go to Amazon.
5. **Evaluation**. The reader browses the selection of thrillers on Amazon to find one that interests them.
6. **Purchase**. The reader buys a book.

Because much of the book market is online, many of these steps now happen in the same place, so the book marketing funnel is much simpler.

At the top of the funnel, you have the Internet. This is where the browsers are—in among the browsers are some people who would be interested in your books, and many more people who aren't interested in your genre; or books at all.

All social media sites are at this level, as well as general and book news sites. Blogs—your blog, fan blogs, and influencer blogs—belong here. So do serial publishing platforms like WattPad and critique blogs like critters.org. Review sites like Goodreads also sit at the wide end of the funnel.

None of these things create raving fans in and of themselves, and none of them are good places to sell books.

```
       The Internet

    Online Bookstores

         Your
       Website(s)
           ?
```

Next in the funnel is the online book market. Its focus is narrower than the Internet because it's a book buyer's market—at least you know these people buy books, and if they like your genre they are also likely to buy your books. This is also the level most unsuccessful indie authors assume is the end of the funnel, because it's a point of purchase. They think, once a book or even several books are up on Amazon and other book sites, that the sales will magically come, and when they don't, the author assumes indie publishing is the problem.

To be successful, you can't view the online book market as an endpoint—each book you publish must also direct readers further down your book marketing funnel.

The narrowest and most important part of the book marketing funnel is your website.

If someone is interested enough to look at your website, they have the potential to become something much more valuable than a person who just bought your book. Your website is your opportunity to turn book buyers into fans.

And I don't mean this in the celebrity sense. I mean the difference between someone who bought a book and a fan is the difference between one sale once and engaging someone who will buy everything you write for years and tell all of their friends.

It's impossible to understate the value of these readers. Statistics show that over 60% of all book sales come from some form of word-of-mouth.

Your website is also where you build trust with potential fans. This is where you put most of your free stuff. You can give out a free anthology, post short stories, provide samples for download, give away a fan newsletter containing interesting news and updates; the list is endless.

Finally, at the bottom of our book marketing funnel, we have… ***a hole.***

Think about it—if a potential fan finds your site and is interested in your work, but they get distracted, or the Internet drops out, or they have no money this week, what is the chance of them ever coming back? What about if someone buys your book on Amazon and likes it, but it's another year before your next book comes out—what are the chances of them finding you again?

Even when they do everything else right, publish good quality books with good blurbs, and have a professional website, most authors forget to plug the hole. Tim Grahl, the author of *Your First 1000 Copies*, calls this the leaky bucket. Authors collect a bucket of readers over time, but they leak out the bottom because the author put nothing in place to keep them.

So how do you plug the hole? With their email address. When you have a reader's email address, you have a way of preventing them from leaking out. You can send them interesting stuff; you can let them know when your next book is coming out; you can send them updates on your current WIP; you can send them deals; and so on.

```
The Internet

Online Bookstores

Your
Website(s)

Reader
Email
```

If you want to be successful as an author, not just an indie author, an email list is non-negotiable.

Remember what I said at the beginning of this chapter: becoming a successful independent publisher is not about selling books, it's about cultivating a fanbase for your work. The volume of sales you make will be directly related to the quality of your email list.

My Four Step Book Marketing System

The book marketing funnel is not just an easy way to visualize how a potential reader passes through your marketing funnel on the way to becoming a fan. It also provides a handy framework for your book marketing process.

This is the four-step marketing process I use with all my books:

1. Reach out to readers who like the things you write about and direct them to your books and your website.
2. Add a Call to Action (CTA) to every book you publish. The CTA directs the reader to either your other books or your website; preferably both.
3. Publish great content on your website that builds trust with your readers and turns them into fans. This does not mean blogging. While blogging can be successful for some, for most of us, it's a waste of time. Great content means new stories and interesting bits from your books, including backstory and world building. For non-fiction authors, this is quality content that supports and promotes your expertise.

4. At every step, look for opportunities to collect an email address so that you can keep in touch with existing and potential fans.

You will learn about each of these steps in much greater detail in Part 2. For now, the most important takeaway is for you to understand that book marketing doesn't have to be complex to be successful.

Simple doesn't mean easy, though. You must work hard at it, but as you will also learn in Part 2, you can automate much of it; freeing you to write.

The Value Funnel

The value funnel is a simple but powerful technique that helps you prioritize your marketing efforts to ensure you spend more time on the things that are the highest value. But first, I am sure you are wondering how much time you should spend on marketing.

The correct answer is "less than the time you spend writing".

Now you might think that's not particularly useful advice, but it depends on your circumstances and goals, so I keep it simple by saying:

The only hard and fast rule of book marketing is you should never spend more time marketing than writing.

Whether you only have a few hours spare a week to write, or you write full-time like me, the number one priority is to make sure you spend most of your available time writing.

If you want ballpark numbers, my view is that, unless you have a major launch in the works, never spend more than two hours a week on marketing, regardless of whether you are a part-timer or write full-time.

Yes, you heard right—two hours a week maximum. And that assumes you have at least 4 hours a week available for your writing—otherwise, do less (or even none).

I am sure you're having a serious WTF?! moment right now, especially if you're unfortunate enough to have been sucked into the "post until your fingers bleed" cult, but I promise you, it's true.

As I wrote earlier in the chapter, I've gone months doing nothing and not seen a drop in sales.

I am writing this early on a Thursday morning. The only marketing I did this week is I spent 40 minutes on Sunday night writing an email announcing a pre-sale of a book I am writing. So far this week that one email has brought in $1200 in pre-sales from a small mailing list and for a book I haven't written yet.

I am not doing anything you couldn't do yourself. All I did was work out that with book marketing, some marketing efforts are much more valuable than others.

And this is where the value funnel comes in, which I like to think of as an inversion of the book marketing funnel. All the broad stuff—social media, etc., are the lowest value, with the value increasing until your mailing list, which is your most valuable marketing asset.

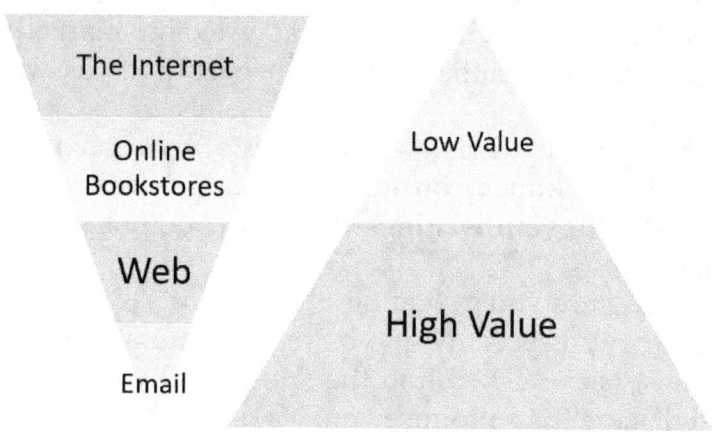

Therefore, the low-value activities are the ones you must spend the least time on, and the high-value activities are the things you need to spend the most time on.

Take a moment to let this sink in.

All the broad-based stuff like social media is low value, so you should be spending the least amount of time on it. Cultivating your mailing list and maintaining your author website is high value, so you should be spending the most amount of time on it.

I bet if you've been drinking the Internet marketing Kool-Aid, you have been doing the opposite of this.

Here's what the data says about email *vs.* social media:

- 6 times as many people will see your email message first thing in the morning compared to a social media post.
- 1.5 times as many people will see your email message during the day.
- Anyone who sees your message is 250 times more likely to engage with the content in an email as the same content in a social media post.
- 77% of people are OK with marketing messages in email. Only 4% appreciate getting marketing messages on social media.

Or to put it another way, when using social media:

You will expend over 2000 times the effort making…
… 20 times as many people hate your guts.

I'm playing with the stats here, but the fact is that on social media, you waste most of your efforts on people who don't care. And even if they care, there is a high likelihood your message will get lost in their feed, and they will never see it.

Even the gurus know social media engagement is very poor, which is why they are always telling you to keep posting and posting and building and building because they know what they're peddling is lousy at converting browsers into readers.

Stats from 2016 show the engagement rate for email was 18%. Guess what it was for Facebook? 0.07%, that's not 0.7%, it's 0.07%. And it's far worse now Facebook is cutting back further on organic reach (to push you to paid advertising) and removing people from your groups if they haven't engaged for a while.

So what are the guru's saying? You must sign up for more accounts and post more often!

Are you freaking kidding me?

Back in my business days, if a sales rep had come to me and said this, I would have told them to go get a better return or go get another job.

You can understand why guru's give this advice—after all, how will they sell their Super-Mega-Secret-Black-White-Hat Social Media Ninja Marketing Course (yours for a bargain five hundred and ninety-seven dollars) if their advice amounted to, "to be honest mate, I think you'd be better off doing something else."

You will do your career a great service to remember the value funnel each time you come across any marketing advice. It can make the difference between wasting huge amounts of time and making $1200 from a 10 line email.

Your Secret Marketing Weapon: WIBBOW?

Once you have got the value funnel clear in your mind, there is one more tool I find handy for getting your priorities right.

Whenever you consider any marketing activity (or any activity that isn't writing), there is a handy acronym I believe all writers should commit to memory:

WIBBOW?

Or,

Would I Be Better Off Writing?

WIBBOW? has been credited to a few people, but its origin is not important—getting into the habit of asking this question every time you start something that isn't writing is important. For example:

- Surfing the net? WIBBOW? For sure
- Browsing my Facebook feed? WIBBOW? Most definitely
- Answering a fan mail? WIBBOW? Maybe—best to keep writing now, and answer emails in a batch this afternoon.

It's an easy habit to get into and, trust me, it makes a huge difference to your productivity!

Just remember it. Make it your mantra.

Would. I. Be. Better. Off. Writing?

WIBBOW?.

I hope you now have a clear view of what your most valuable marketing activities are, and an idea of how to prioritize them. In Part 2, I will show you the exact process for putting the value funnel and WIBBOW? into practice.

Taming the Social Media Beast

In Part 2, I will show you how to use social media effectively, but given we are talking about marketing and managing time in this chapter, I thought I would finish with a few pointers on taming the social media beast, so it's not such a huge time sink.

I am not against authors using social media, but there is no good evidence social media helps new authors—at least in the way it's most often used. Social media is valuable as a great way to keep in touch with your existing fans as your success grows, but if you are spending any more than an hour or two a week on social media when you could write, you are most likely doing your career more harm than good.

To get you on the right track, here are my top 10 ways to tame the social media beast:

1. Pick one social media platform as your primary channel. It doesn't matter which one, but it's a good idea to start with the one you are most comfortable with.

2. Direct all other social media accounts to your primary channel.

3. Have a separate author account to your personal account on all channels you will use as your author self.

4. Only post useful content about your work. Re-posting other people's stuff is a waste of your time.
5. Use Other People's Lists (OPL). I will explain how to use OPL in Part 2.
6. It's OK to promote your books, just not every day.
7. Delete all social media apps from your phone.
8. Set a time for outreach. I'll teach you effective outreach techniques in Part 2
9. Set a time for wasting time. We're all human after all—downtime is good.
10. Ask WIBBOW? every time you reach for social media.

PART 2

YOUR INDIE PUBLISHING MACHINE

Chapter 6
The Indie Publishing Machine

As I explained in Part 1 of the book, cultivating an active, long-term fan base for your work is key to becoming a successful independent publisher.

However, building a substantial body of work is also critical, so you need to develop a balance between time spent growing and managing your fan base and writing time.

The challenge is not identifying the things that waste our time (e.g., surfing the net) when we should be writing. We can all identify those—even if we sometimes lack the willpower to stop.

The challenge is identifying which, among a range of things you can do, benefit your career the most. Lucky for us, we can make this challenge easier if we apply a simple principle humans have understood for around 200 years—the Pareto Principle.

The Pareto Principle, or 80/20 Rule, states that 80% of the effects come from 20% of the causes. This is not some trendy business-speak—we have had a solid understanding of the 80/20 Rule since the 19th century. It applies to human endeavors and many natural phenomena.

Applied to indie publishing, the 80/20 Rule says that 80% of an author's success comes from 20% of their efforts. The corollary to this is 80% of your efforts are wasted for little gain.

Which brings us to the two core principles of the Indie Publishing Machine.

To be a successful author with maximum writing time, you must:

1. Identify the activities that bring you the most value (the 20%); and
2. Automate these activities as much as possible.

Principle 1 is the most difficult. Identifying the 20%—the essential few activities that give you most of your results—are not obvious at first, and it can take some time to work out what works for you.

Through trial and error, and through researching successful strategies used by other independent authors, I have discovered there are few things important to establishing a successful writing career. These essentials form the core of the Indie Publishing Machine—a system that puts these high-value activities into practice.

The Indie Publishing Machine has four essential parts:

1. Outreach content
2. Your books available for sale on Amazon
3. A professional author website; and
4. A mailing list

These are the essential few; the four things that only require 20% of your effort but will give you 80% of your results. You can automate much of these essential parts and once set up, they are simple to maintain; giving you more free time to write.

Set up right, your Indie Publishing Machine will make money for you 24/7 every day of the year, with minimal input from you. It still takes effort to set up, and you must keep writing books, so there's nothing magical or get rich quick going on here.

The technical parts of your Indie Publishing Machine are simple to create, even if you're all thumbs with technology. In the remaining chapters of the book, I will show you how to set up each of these four essential parts.

If you are not great with technology or don't want to get your hands dirty with the technical side of your Indie Publishing Machine, the last chapter of the book shows you where you can go to hire techies for reasonable rates.

How it Works

Remember in Part 1 how I said the immutable math of publishing is to be successful you must:

A. Write more books; and
B. Sell more of your existing books?

I appreciate this is obvious, but what separates successful authors from the rest is they understand that A (writing more books) is much more important than B (selling more books). This is because writing more books leads to selling more books with minimal extra effort from you.

Let me illustrate with an example. The conventional advice goes like this:

1. Publish a book
2. Market the heck out of the book
3. Repeat

While this is compelling and straightforward advice, what actually happens is the author:

1. Markets the heck out of the book
2. Nothing happens
3. Repeats until author goes insane or gives up

This is because the conventional advice does nothing to answer the trust question I wrote about in Chapter 5. You can yell "Buy my book!" from every rooftop in the land, but it won't make any difference because nobody cares.

I don't state this to be miserable and negative but as a fact. Think about it—you are one voice in the thousand a potential reader will hear today, and if they don't know you and trust you, the chances of them caring about what you have to say is near zero.

The Indie Publishing Machine turns this thinking on its head by accepting that until a reader trusts you, marketing your book to them is a waste of time.

With the Indie Publishing Machine, you:

1. Publish a book
2. Update your other books and content, so they link to your new book
3. Repeat

Note there is no mention of marketing. Remember what I said in Chapter 5? You do not "sell" books, nor are you trying to make people buy your book—you are putting it out there in the market and making it easier to find for those who are already looking for a book just like yours.

Once they've read one of your books (or any other piece of content you wrote), and trust you, the links provide the reader a pathway to your other work. This linking—where each piece of your content links to one or more other works—is not only organic marketing best-practice, but it's also incredibly effective for books.

And it explains why writing more books is much more important than trying to sell more books, because the more books and content you have out there, the more of these organic links you will collect, and your books will sell more with no additional effort from you.

Like all things, it is possible to overdo it and reduce its effectiveness (not to mention waste a lot of time), so getting back to the 80/20 rule, this is what I find to be the most effective implementation of the Indie Publishing Machine:

- Your outreach content (wide end of the funnel) directs potential fans to a landing page on your website that provides valuable, free content in exchange for an email address.
- Every book you have for sale on Amazon has a Call to Action (CTA) in the front and in the back that directs the reader to a landing page on your website that provides valuable, free content in exchange for an email address. This content does not need to be different from the content for Internet browsers.
- Your website home page has links to the landing pages for the above free content.
- Your website lists all your published books, with links to Amazon.
- Your website lists the current book you are working on, and forthcoming titles, with a waiting list sign-up form.
- Your website also has a sign-up form where people can join your newsletter.

Keeping your Indie Publishing Machine running is easy; it should not take any more than a few hours a month. All you need to do is:

- Post outreach content (e.g., social media posts, blog posts, articles, a new story on your website—the list is endless). You decide how much you want to post,

but try to be consistent.
- Send one or two emails a month to your mailing list.
- Answer any queries you get from your readers.
- Update your book catalog when you have a new book available.

And that's it. I know, you might wonder how it could be so simple, but honestly, this is all you need to get that 80% return.

You can and will add to this over time, but to get started on a successful writing career, this is all you need. Remember WIBBOW?—your writing will always be more important.

That's it for this chapter. In the next chapter, I will teach you how to implement an effective outreach program. Outreach is your number 1 tool for engaging and building trust with potential readers and turning them into life-long fans.

Chapter 7
Outreach

The term outreach is used to describe a range of marketing activities, so for the sake of clarity, this is how I define outreach:

Outreach is any activity designed to direct people interested in the type of books you write further down your book marketing funnel.

These activities must satisfy one criterion to be outreach:

Does it link to either your website or to a bio that links to your website?

If the answer is "No", then it's not called outreach—it's called Wasting Your Time.

Take your time to absorb this distinction because it's vital to your success. Outreach is action-oriented. Your goal is to build trust with the reader. If your outreach content doesn't encourage a potential fan to take action towards building trust, you are wasting your time.

The purpose of outreach is to build trust with potential readers and turn them into fans.

Outreach must link to your author website. To be more specific, that link must go to a page offering great free content. This can be a promo giving something away in return for an email address, or free content related to the linking content.

For example, you publish a short article on another blog site that links back to the full article on your website. For fiction authors, this could be an excerpt from a new short story linking back to the whole story. In these examples, the Call to Action (CTA) can be a newsletter sign-up form embedded in the content or a free PDF download of the complete article or story.

If your content links to a sales page—either on Amazon or a sales page on your website—it's not outreach, it's advertising.

Advertising is a different beast to outreach, with different goals. Remember, outreach is for building trust, and advertising is for generating sales. Advertising can work for authors, but it's unnecessary for your success, regardless of what some might say. The reason for this is ads only work while the ads are running.

Whereas with outreach, you are building permanent organic links to your work. As organic growth outperforms paid growth on every platform online, ads should never be your main marketing strategy.

After all, which book are you more likely to buy—the one that keeps popping up in your feed, no matter how many times you have tried to silence it, or the one recommended by a friend over your morning coffee?

Outreach is Active

Outreach is the active part of your book marketing.

Your books and the links they contain, articles and stories on your site, and social media author pages are passive marketing. They're all content you don't often change once they're published.

Effective outreach requires you to seek opportunities to draw readers into your books. Most often, this comprises creating and sharing content. It can also be simple things like making sure your signature block in emails and online forums contain a link to your website.

Outreach Content is Sharable

Remember what I said in Chapter 5: growth happens when you create content users want to share. So, to improve the effectiveness of your outreach, any content you produce should also be easy to share.

Sharability is where effective social media use becomes an important part of your outreach.

No, I am not contradicting myself here—I still believe social media is low value, and your time is better spent elsewhere. The key word here is "effective".

While social media is unnecessary for you to succeed, its sheer size as a source of potential readers makes it important for you to understand effective social media use can be valuable.

To be effective with social media outreach, you must distinguish between "sharing content" and "content that is easy to share".

Emailing your fans and posting the same message on your Facebook page are both sharing content.

How easy it is for the recipient to share the message governs the sharability of each message.

A Facebook post is easy to share by default, but it's of low value to you. The email is orders of magnitude more valuable, but how do you make it easy to share? By putting social share buttons in the email, of course!

You can make your high-value content easy to share by adding social sharing capability, for example:

- Add social share buttons to each of your articles or blog posts
- Put "Click to Tweet" scripts in your articles
- Add a pin to an infographic or relevant screenshot or artwork
- Enable Facebook comments on your posts

Other People's Lists (OPL)

You can improve the effectiveness of social media outreach by employing the concept of *Other People's Lists* or OPL, which I introduced in Chapter 5.

Your reach is limited—whether it be your author website or your author feed on whatever social media platforms you use. This is acute on the most popular social media platforms as they limit your organic reach to push you to paid advertising.

With OPL, you're not sharing the content. All you need to do is create something awesome, and make it easy for others to share with their list.

This is the real secret sauce the guru's never tell you about. It isn't the gazillion posts *you* created that brings the success, it's the few great posts in the gazillion *someone else* shared that brings the success.

What's super cool about this, is that you don't even have to be on a particular platform for this to work—people will share your good stuff on their favorite platform for you.

Two examples from my work:

1. I get a substantial amount of organic traffic to my computer programming website from Quora, Reddit and Stack Overflow despite not having accounts with any of them or having ever posted a single piece of content on these sites. This traffic is all from users of these forums posting links to my work.
2. I get a non-trivial amount of traffic from Twitter, even though I have never sent a tweet. This traffic comes from Twitter users tweeting links to my content.

You still have to create content that's good enough to share. However, you can spend all the time you save by not posting yourself into exhaustion creating a few pieces of outstanding content and making them easy to share.

There is also another aspect to OPL you can leverage to improve your reach.

On balance, it's more effective to post content on external websites or media platforms. Note, I say on balance—it isn't always more effective, but broadly speaking:

- It's better to post or share content in a social media group than it is to share in your personal feed.
- It's better to publish an article on a related blog or news site than it is to post on your site.
- It's better to have a story published in collaboration with other authors than publishing an anthology of your stories.

There are no hard and fast rules here—what works for one author, may not work for another. The underlying principle is it's better to find an existing audience for a particular piece of content than to try and create an audience for the content. You should keep this in mind when you are planning your outreach.

Being SMART With Outreach

SMART is an acronym often used in vocational education and in self-help literature as a tool for setting effective goals.

It stands for *Specific, Measurable, Achievable, Realistic* and *Time-limited*.

What it means is for any goal to be effective, it must be:

1. Explicit;
2. You must have a measure of success or failure;
3. You must feel like its achievable;
4. It must be possible to achieve; and
5. It must have a deadline.

For outreach, I have simplified this to the *Who*, *What*, *Where*, *When* and *Why* or 5Ws of outreach activities.

You should be able to see straight away, why this is so effective in laser targeting your marketing efforts and eliminating time wasters.

Let's look at the conventional approach to social media marketing in terms of the 5Ws:

- **Who?** Everyone!
- **What?** Um, memes are popular, aren't they?
- **Where?** Is there such a thing as too many social accounts?
- **When?** RIGHT NOW! Because, like, it's *super* important. Right?
- **Why?** Because everyone else is doing it, silly!

OK, so I'm going somewhat over the top here, but we're all guilty of being vague with our intentions and expectations. You can't run a successful business without specific goals. Of all the positive things you can do for your writing career, having specific marketing goals is second only to specific writing goals.

So, here's a better example of the 5Ws:

- **Who?** Readers of fast-paced, short sci-fi
- **What?** A new flash fiction story
- **Where?** Publish on my website then post a link to the story in Facebook sci-fi groups
- **When?** May 27th
- **Why?** Add 50 new readers to my mailing list

Here's another one:

- **Who?** Readers of YA thrillers
- **What?** Guest blog post
- **Where?** The YA thrillers website
- **When?** July 1st
- **Why?** Increase weekly traffic to my website by 10%

You get the idea.

Let's explore the 5Ws in more detail, so you get a better understanding of what makes a great outreach activity.

Who

Who should be as specific as possible. There is no point targeting "sci-fi readers" or "fantasy readers" or "romance readers" because those terms are far too broad. To allow you to sort the browsers from someone who is likely to become a fan, you need to be more specific. "cyberpunk dystopian romance lovers" is far more likely to help you direct your efforts to the right readers if you write cyberpunk dystopian romance.

What

What is the content itself. It can be everything from a short post to an entire book. It's not limited to text either—What includes photo's, infographics, drawings, and dare I say it, memes.

Where

Where is the platform. Where can be social media, your website, or any other website.

As Calls to Action (CTAs) can be outreach, Where can also be promotions and giveaways in one of your books, magazines or in an anthology you create with other authors. Just remember ads and outreach are different—outreach directs people to free stuff, ads direct people to stuff they have to pay for.

When

When doesn't need much explanation, it's the date of publication.

Why?

Why is the most important of the 5Ws because it's how you measure success or failure.

Why must provide an objective measure of success.

So, if you go back to my last example, "Increase weekly traffic" would not have been an acceptable Why because it's not an objective measure. "Increase weekly traffic by 10%" is measurable. You can look at your analytics and make a clear decision. Yes, it did, or no, it didn't.

Make Better Marketing Decisions

Remember the marketing reset exercise we did in Chapter 5?
Now you have a tool to measure the level of outreach success. When you do a periodic review of your outreach efforts, rather than going with your gut, you can confidently identify the activities that brought you the most benefit.
In combination, What and Where cover the gamut of book marketing. "What is the best way to promote my books?" is the number one question I get asked. This question has spawned millions of "How to …" articles, and selling the current trendiest answer to the question is how the Internet marketing gurus make their money. When there are so many thousands of options, it's easy to see why authors get overwhelmed.

There is no one best way, and what is best for me might not be best for you because your audience is different. Which is why conducting the 5Ws with every outreach activity is so important.

The Indie Publishing Machine is about concentrating on the 20% of efforts that bring 80% of your results, but when you first start, you don't know what the 20% is. Once you have a clear objective (your goal or your Why) you will learn which things work best for you.

I won't leave you on your own, though. From personal experience and research, I know there are a few channels and approaches that have a universal application for authors and should be a part of your 20%.

I have included a bonus chapter at the end of the book called "Outreach FAQ" that answers common questions regarding blogs, advertising, book launches, and several other marketing related questions.

Prioritize Outreach Activities

Before I go on to the next chapter, I want to draw your attention back to the Value Funnel, which I covered in Chapter 5.

Outreach is marketing, so you must complete it within whatever timeframe you have allocated for marketing during the week; remember, marketing time must never exceed writing time.

Given limited hours available, and the almost unlimited outreach options available, prioritizing activities is very important.

On the value spectrum, social media is the least valuable and cultivating your email list is the most; with Amazon and your website coming somewhere in the middle. Given a list of activities, the Value Funnel helps you complete them in priority order.

Say, for example, you have a Facebook post and an email you have done your 5Ws for and are ready to go, but you only have time for one task. The Value Funnel says the email is the most important, so you send it first. You publish the Facebook post if you find more time later, or you can schedule it into next week's marketing.

How about if you have a book description and keywords that need updating on Amazon and the same Facebook post? The book description and keywords get done because they're more important than the post.

If, on the other hand, you have an email to go out and the book description update, then the email takes precedent. And so on.

OK, that wraps it up for outreach. The remaining chapters in the book cover the technical setup of your mailing list, your author website, and publishing your books on Amazon. And for the technically challenged, don't panic—the final chapter shows you how to find techies to do all the hard stuff for you.

Images hard to read?

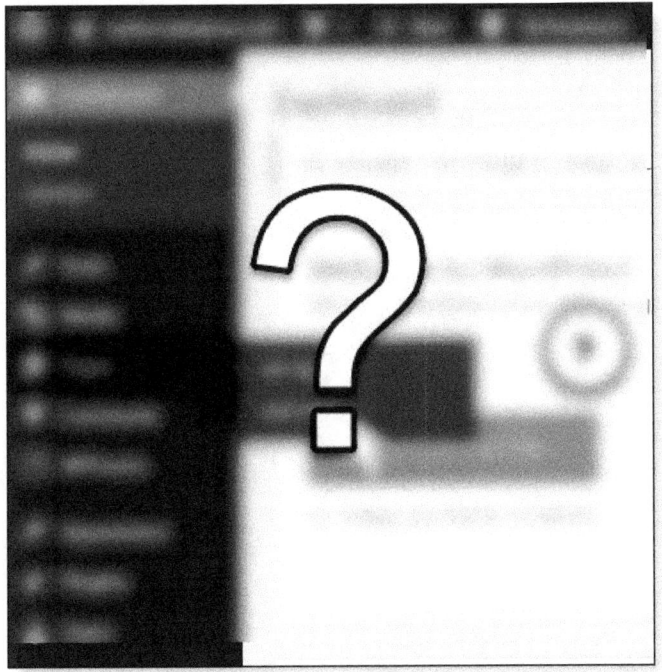

Download all the images from the book in high resolution for viewing on a tablet, laptop or desktop.

Download from http://bit.ly/SPS01bonus.

Chapter 8
Create Your Mailing List

In this chapter, I will show you how to set up your mailing list software.

A mailing list is a must if you want to build a successful indie publishing business. Unfortunately, this is not as simple as keeping a list of email addresses and using your email software to send out newsletters to your list.

Because of global anti-SPAM laws, sending to any more than a hundred recipients at a time is likely to get your email account suspended.

It's also difficult to manage a mailing list manually.

Mailing list software solves this problem by providing a platform compliant with anti-SPAM laws, while also providing a convenient way to manage a large list of contacts. As most marketers use mailing lists, it's also quite a lucrative business—so there are hundreds of companies offering mailing list software. These offerings range from free to many hundreds and even thousands of dollars a month.

For authors who are starting with their indie publishing business, my advice is simple:

1. The mailing list software should be free or low cost; and
2. It mustn't require a developer to set up.

The first criterion is the most important for new authors. It may be months, even years before you make enough money from your books to cover the cost of a mailing list subscription.

Unless you have another income where you can cover the cost, finding the money each month for another subscription is a stress that Creative Brain doesn't need.

Unfortunately, free and low-cost services attract lots of spammers, so you run into issues of deliverability. If you are emailing from a server that has a history of sending low quality and spam email, your emails risk being sent straight to the spam folder or not being delivered at all.

When you are starting, I recommend MailChimp's free account. MailChimp is not the best list management software, but it has one stand out feature perfect for new authors: you can have up to 2000 subscribers before you must pay for a subscription.

Other vendors also offer free accounts, but they're more limited in functionality, managed by overseas companies with poor deliverability or need a developer to set up.

MailChimp's free account limits you to collecting names into one list and sending out newsletters and updates, but this is still better than no list at all. You also get no support from MailChimp unless you pay, but the list is easy to export to a paid account once you have enough income to justify the subscription.

I don't explain how to set up a paid account in this book, as it doesn't meet the first criteria.

If you are curious, I don't use or recommend MailChimp for paid accounts. I use ConvertKit for all my professional accounts. As ConvertKit is designed for creators, it's a superior solution for creating more sophisticated workflows suitable for authors.

Set up MailChimp

Signing up for MailChimp is easy—first, jump over to your favorite browser and search for MailChimp, or type "https://mailchimp.com" into the address bar.

1. Once you are on the MailChimp homepage, click on the **Sign Up Free** button.

2. MailChimp will prompt you to enter an email

address, username, and password to create your account.

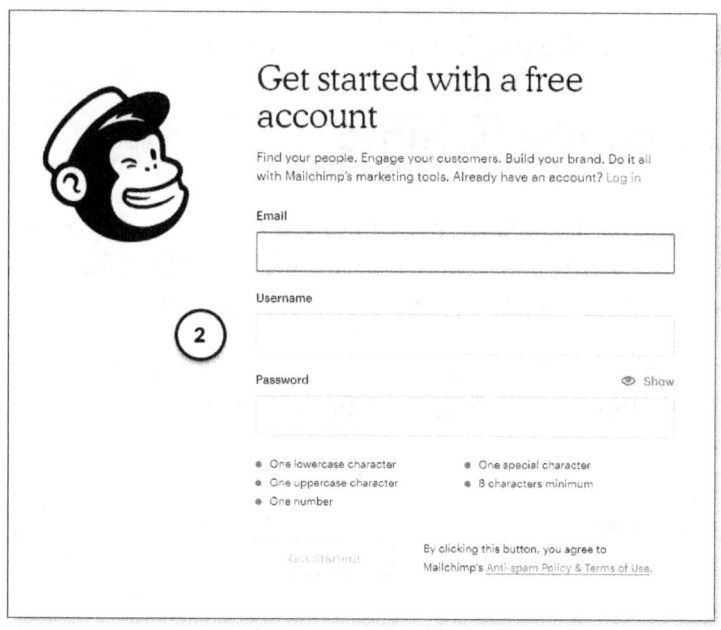

You will need to verify your email to activate your MailChimp account.

3. Select the **Free** account.

CREATE YOUR MAILING LIST   113

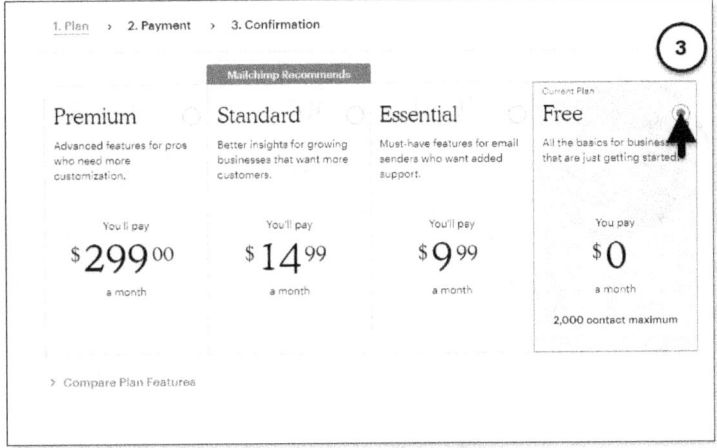

4. You then get taken to the sign-up interview. Enter your name and company information. If you haven't set up a company for your writing, the business name can be your name. Enter the address for your author website. If you haven't set up your author website yet, you can enter a Facebook or Twitter URL (screenshot on next page).

5. Next, you need to enter your physical address. For your emails to comply with international SPAM laws, this must be a valid address for you or your business. This can be a problem for authors because most of us don't have a business address. Why it's a problem, is that if you put your home address in here, MailChimp will attach it to every email you send. For privacy reasons, this is something you don't want to do.

The solution to this problem is simple: most countries offer post office boxes or private mailboxes for reasonable yearly rates. For your privacy, you should get one of these. If you haven't got one yet, put whatever address you like in here. MailChimp won't stop you if you put in a bogus address, and it's easy to change later.

Remember though, if you send any emails without a legitimate address, you run a high risk of having your account suspended—so, you must enter a valid address before you send your first email.

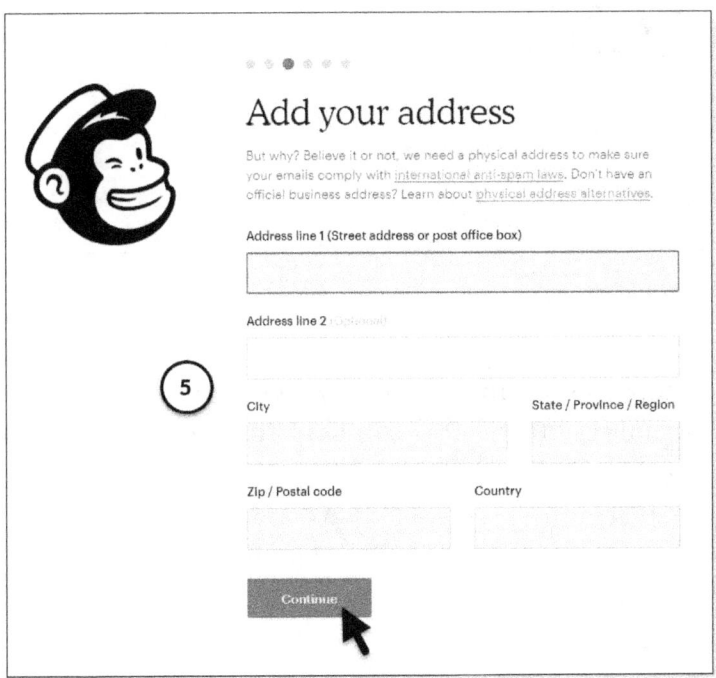

The rest of the sign-up interview comprises a series of questions MailChimp will use to configure your account:

- First it will ask you if you have a subscriber list to upload. In most cases, this will be no.

- Then MailChimp will want you to connect some social accounts. You can skip this and set them up later.

CREATE YOUR MAILING LIST 117

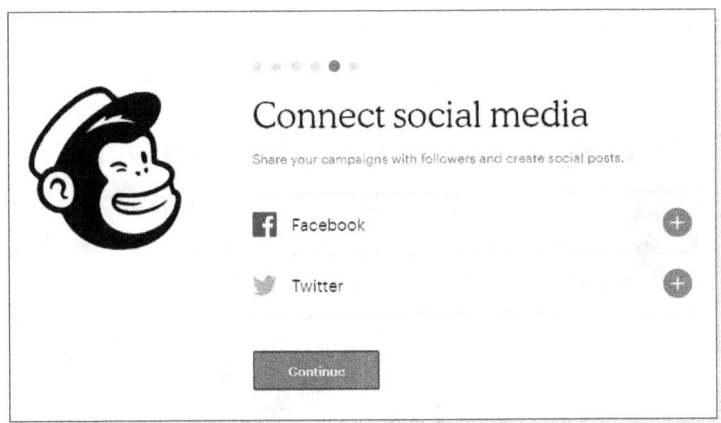

- Most of the marketing path questions you won't know the answer to yet, so best to click "Not right now".

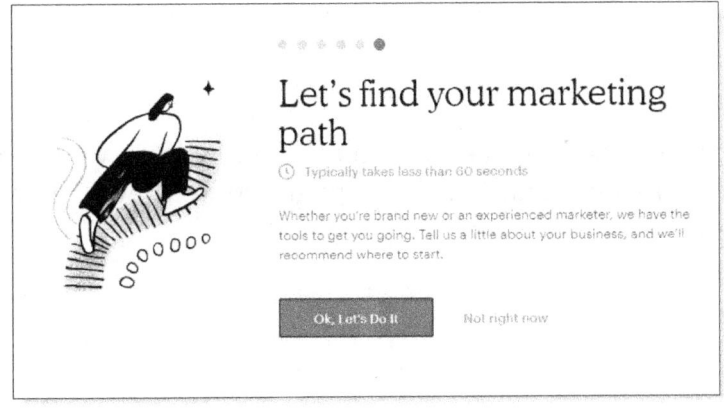

- You also don't want their recommended bundle, it's an up-sell you don't need.

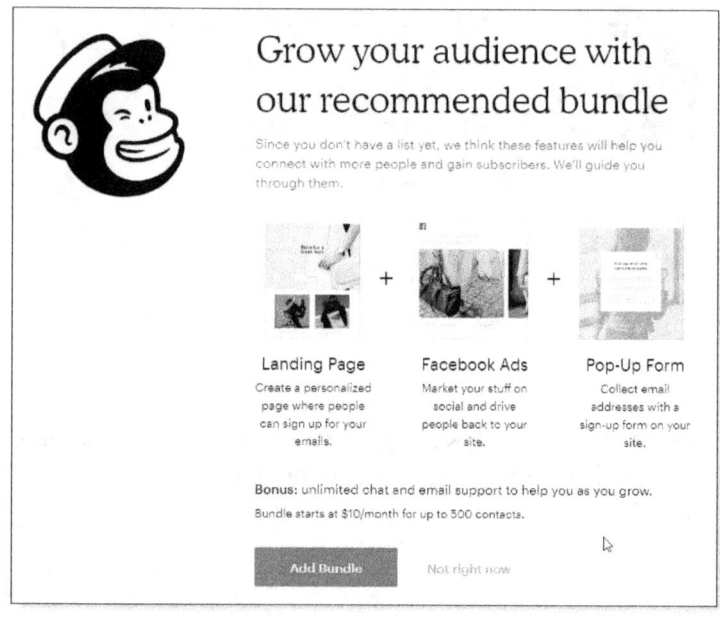

- Click the **Let's Go** button and MailChimp will take you to yet another setup page where they nag you for more information.

Create Your Mailing List

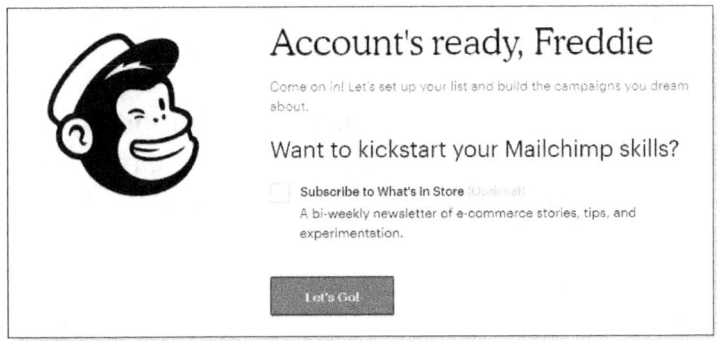

- Ignore the bonus—this is the same up-sell you canceled before, click on "Go to my dashboard".

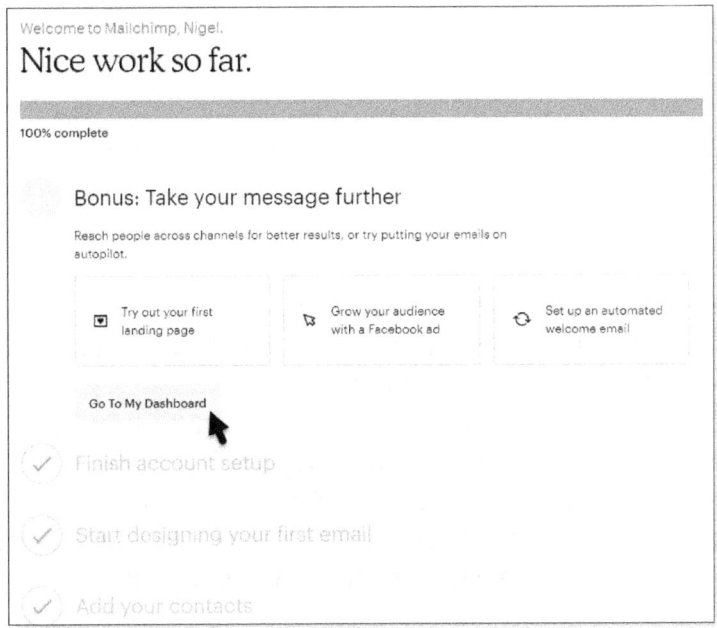

- Click "Not right now" to the marketing recommendations because they are another up-sell.

    6. Once the up-sell message disappears, your MailChimp dashboard should be clear, and your shiny new MailChimp account is ready to go.

The downside to MailChimp's free account is they will constantly try to up-sell you. This can be annoying, but in most cases, it's easy to ignore.

The only things you will use MailChimp for is sign-up forms for your newsletter and creating waiting lists for your books—all of which are free to use on MailChimp until you get 2000 subscribers. I will show you how to set up each of these in Chapter 10.

Before I move on, I want to point out one other good thing about MailChimp.

7. What MailChimp gets right is its extensive, easy-to-read help.

    If you scroll to the bottom of your dashboard, you can see links to new features in MailChimp, marketing guides, and a comprehensive knowledge base with guides, tutorials and technical information.

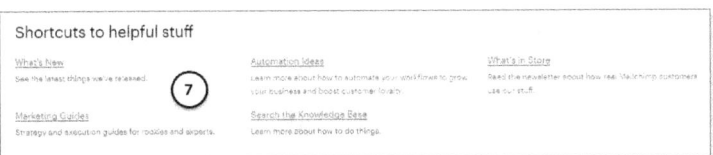

You will find these resources useful as you learn more about MailChimp and email list management.

Chapter 9

Your Author Website: Host and Domain Setup

Setting up your author website can be a challenge, especially for authors who are not confident with technology.

If you've researched setting up a website before, it's also likely you felt overwhelmed by the thousands of options available.

If you are not technical or feel overwhelmed—don't worry because I will make this easy for you.

If you get to the end of the next few chapters, and the technology still feels like dipping your hand into a pocket full of spiders, remember the last chapter in the book shows you where you can find techies to do it all for you.

I only have one recommendation for author websites—a self-hosted WordPress site, hosted on WPX Hosting.

That's it. See how easy that was?

OK, that needs more explaining.

A self-hosted site gives you complete control over the web server that runs your site. This means you have full administrator access to your registered domain, the hosting account, and the WordPress installation for your website.

The alternative to self-hosted is offered by the likes of Weebly, Wix, Squarespace, and many others trying to lock you into their platform.

It's this last point why I recommend that you should never go with a hosted platform—because once you are on a platform you're locked in, and it can be impossible to get off without rebuilding your site. I've gone through this process with at least a dozen clients over the years, and trust me, it's not something you want to do.

You are an author, and authors are in for the long haul. Hosted platforms come and go. The extra bit of work you need to do to have total control over your author platform will pay for itself multiple times because you won't need to change platforms and redo everything every few years.

Self-hosting takes more effort to set up, but modern web hosts make setting up a website more straightforward with automatic installation and configuration of website software.

Which brings me to the next point—why WPX Hosting?

I've worked in IT on and off for 25 years and have used more hosts than I can count.

If you do any research, you will find the only thing more numerous than web hosting companies is opinions on web hosting companies.

This can be confusing if you are not a technical person, so let me make it as simple as I can.

A web host is a computer; similar to the one sitting on your desk. Your website is a program running on this computer. Web hosting companies buy or lease lots of computers so they can run lots of sites. They rent space on the computers to people like you and me so that we can run our websites.

The cost of computers and website support doesn't vary much across the world, so the price you pay depends on how many other websites the host runs on one computer.

A cheap host will run lots of websites on a single computer. An expensive host will only run a few, or even just one.

So, if you buy a $50 per year hosting account, there is a high chance that the host will install your author website on the same computer as hundreds of others. And what happens when you open too many apps on your computer? That's right—everything runs slower and sometimes an app crashes (or even the whole computer!).

The cheaper the host, the slower and less reliable it will be. This might not be a problem while your author site has minimal traffic, but as you grow, it can create huge headaches. What you need is a hosting company that strikes a balance between not breaking the bank when you start and being powerful enough to grow with you.

At $25 a month (or $250 a year) WPX hosting is neither cheap nor expensive. WPX is rock solid, fast, comes with excellent support and is competitively priced for the performance it offers. I have paid more for less with other hosts, so I recommend it as it strikes that critical balance between price and power.

If you already have a website, or $25 a month is too much, it's OK. Sometimes we have to take baby steps, so don't think you have to change everything at once.

The WordPress setup works on any host with an automatic installer for WordPress 5. Adding content to WordPress is the same regardless of who is hosting the site, and if your existing website is not WordPress, only the content editor will be different. The content you add to your site is the same.

As for WordPress? I recommend it because it's everywhere and it is easy to use if you ignore the parts you don't need. Because it's everywhere, it also has excellent support and a large community of resources for you to access.

An author website is not complex to build, but there is quite a lot to do, so I have broken the process into three chapters:

1. In this chapter, I show you how to create your hosting account and register your domain.
2. In Chapter 10, I show you how to install and set up your WordPress site; and
3. In Chapter 11, I show you how to add the content to your site.

Please note that the next three chapters are not a WordPress tutorial. I show you how to add what I believe to be the minimum content necessary for an author website, without going into detail on the content blocks and editing tools available in WordPress.

If you want to learn more about WordPress, there is no shortage of free tutorials available online.

This is the only chapter in the book where you need to spend money (assuming you don't already have a website). You will need a valid debit or credit Visa or Mastercard to complete the sign-up process.

At the time of writing, it costs $11 to register the domain, and the hosting account is $25 a month. That's US dollars for those of you who aren't in the US. You can save money by paying your hosting account yearly, but that costs $249.99 up front.

Create a Hosting Account

Jump over to the WPX Hosting website by either searching for "WPX hosting" in your favorite browser, or going to "https://wpxhosting.com".

When you get to their site, the first thing I want you to note is the little guy down in the bottom right corner (screenshot on next page).

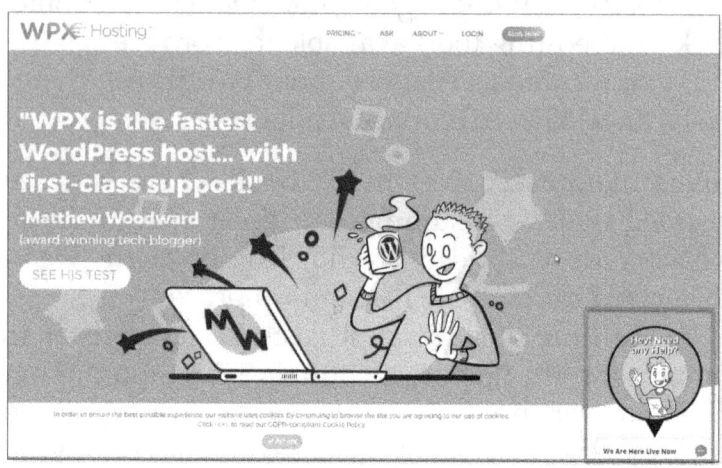

If you click on the live chat icon, you can open a chat window with a real person.

They promise a response within 30 seconds, and they live up to the promise: I have started chats with them at all hours of the day, and they never take long to answer.

Whoever trains their support staff is a wizard. I have never worked with more knowledgeable, patient, and professional support staff before—even from hosts charging much more money per month.

The chat box pops up on every page on their site. Do not be afraid to use it when you get stuck. If you tell them you are not technical, they will even do a lot of the more difficult tasks for you for free.

1. Click on "Pricing" in the top menu, then select domains to go to the domain search page.

You should always try to buy a domain name that is the same as the name you put on your books. So, if you publish under the name Sarah J. Smith, try to buy "sarahjsmith.com".

2. To search for a domain with your name, type your name into the search bar. For this example, I will use "Joe Smith" as my author name.

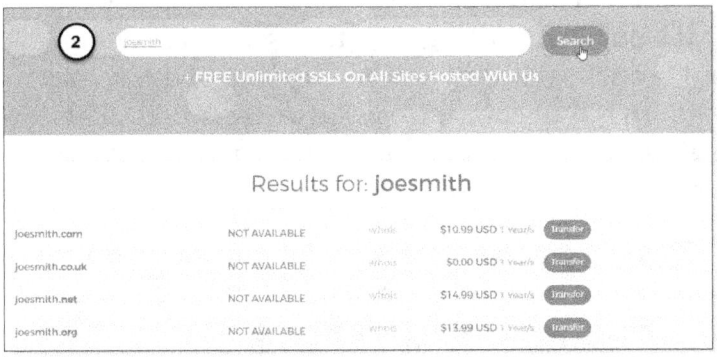

You can see that Joe Smith is popular as far as names go.

If you scroll down the page, you can see some Joe Smith domains are available, but always try to get a ".com" or a ".net" domain.

This is where you can try a little trick if your name is already registered as a domain. Try your name with "author" on the end. So with our popular Mr. Smith, let's try "joesmithauthor".

Results for: joesmithauthor			
joesmithauthor.com	AVAILABLE	$10.99 USD 1 Year/s	Register
joesmithauthor.co.uk	AVAILABLE	$8.99 USD 1 Year/s	Register
joesmithauthor.net	AVAILABLE	$14.99 USD 1 Year/s	Register
joesmithauthor.org	AVAILABLE	$13.99 USD 1 Year/s	Register

Success!

You can see, even with a common name like Joe Smith, you can still find a suitable domain to register.

If you were only going to register a domain, you could click the big green register button next to joesmithauthor.com, but we won't do that. This exercise was to find a suitable domain name available for purchase. We'll register the domain in the next step.

3. Click on the **Start Now** button at the top of your browser window, and WPX will take you to the managed hosting sales page.

Author Website - Host and Domain Setup

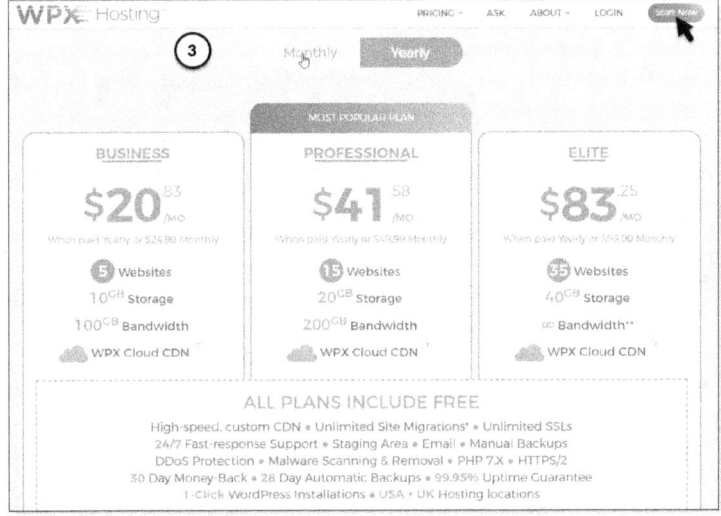

Ignore the "most popular" plan; you won't need a plan that large with an author site. Notice that the page opens with the yearly plan selected. Remember, it might say just over $20 a month, but you'll pay for the whole year up front. You can ignore the monthly or yearly billing selection for now; you get to choose your billing preferences later in the sign-up process.

Scroll down and click the **Get Started** button. Click **Host in USA**.

4. Select "I need a new domain + Hosting" (screenshot on next page).

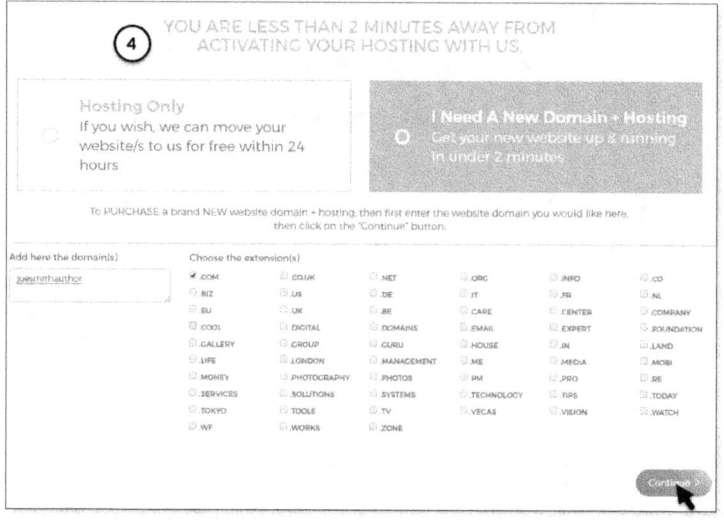

- Enter the domain you selected a minute ago in the box that appears below. Note that you can select the ".net" domain and other top-level domains, but for this example, I will stick with the ".com". Click on **Continue**.

   5. Note that WPX has verified your domain name is available. Click on **Order Now**.

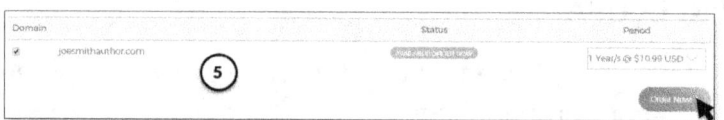

6. Leave the Nameservers and Domain contacts as they are, and click **Continue**.

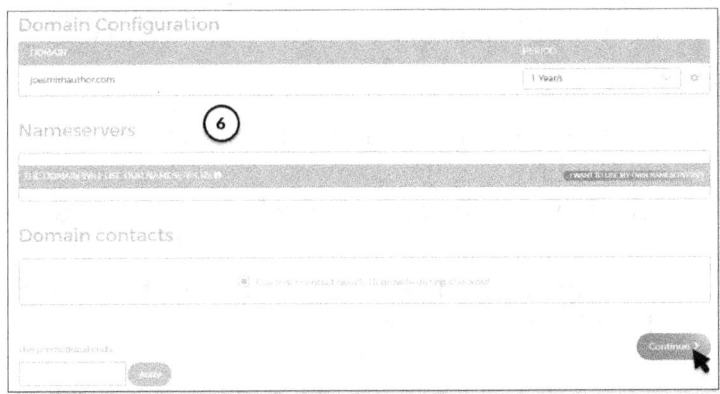

7. Select monthly or yearly billing and then click **Continue**.

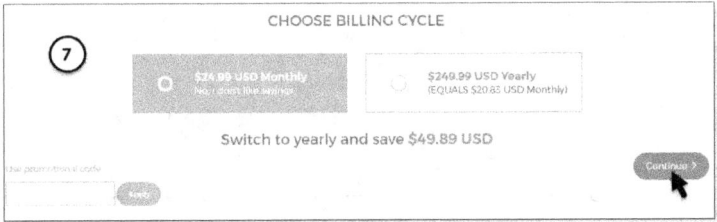

Next is the payment page. Once WPX processes the payment, your domain registration is complete.

Configure Your Domain

Before we move on to setting up your author website, there are a couple more things you need to do with the domain.

> 8. First, click on the "Domains" menu at the top of the browser to go to your registered domains page. You will see your new domain listed in the domain table. Go over to the blue gear icon on the right of the row, and select "Registrar Lock" (screenshot on next page).

You want to set it to ON. The registrar lock ensures that no-one can steal your domain name from you if you ever forget to renew it by the due date.

Author Website - Host and Domain Setup

9. Second, you need to point your domain name at your web server. Every website on the Internet has an address, just like the house you live in has an address. Because your domain name is new, it doesn't point to the physical address of your website.

   To fix this requires some cut and paste. Go back to your WPX dashboard and click on "WordPress Hosting". Click on **Manage all sites on this account**.

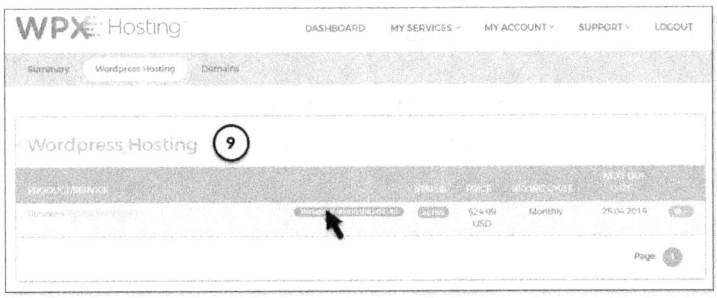

- Under "Server Details", note the entries next to Nameserver 1 and Nameserver 2. Nameservers are like a local address book for the host. They point domain names to the physical website hosted on their servers.

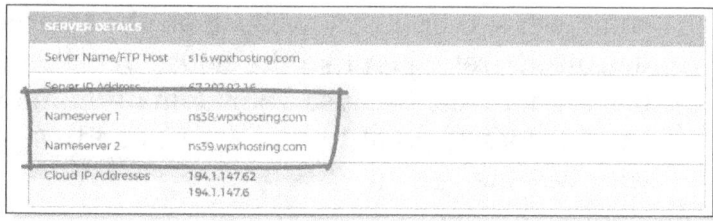

- Go back to the dashboard menu and open the "Domains" link in another tab or window. What you want is your hosting page open the same time as your domains page so you can copy and paste from one to the other.

    10. Select your new domain name and scroll down to the Nameservers list. Click on **Manage Nameservers**.

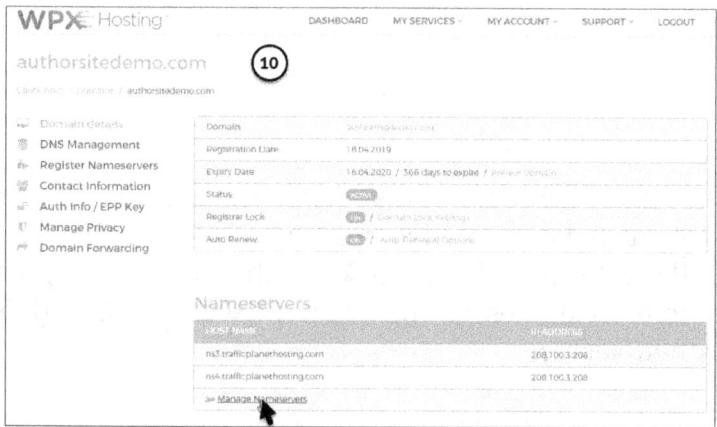

- Change "General settings" to CUSTOM and delete all the current records.
- Copy the Nameserver 1 and Nameserver 2 addresses from your hosting account to your domain name. Don't worry about the Nameserver IP addresses; they will update automatically.
- Click **Save Changes**.

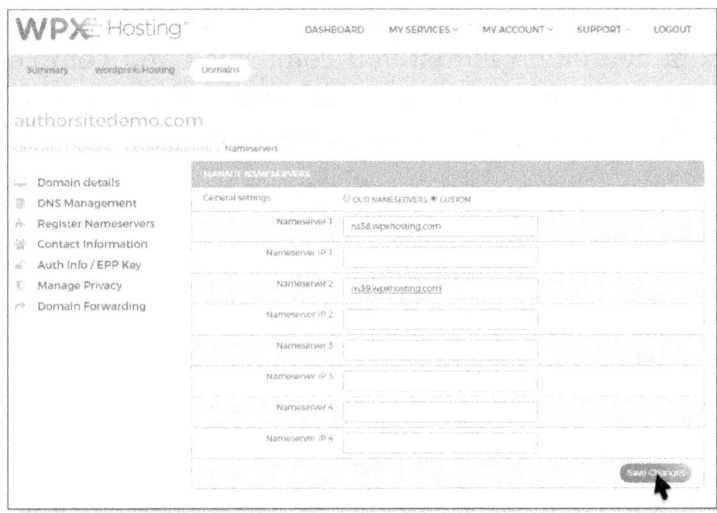

Now you have to wait. The Internet is a global network—you have linked your domain name to your physical web address, but the rest of the Internet doesn't know that yet.

This is where the Domain Name Service or DNS takes over. The DNS tells the rest of the world you have created a new website. Think of the DNS as your robot messenger that updates everyone's address book for you automatically.

As you can appreciate, this takes time. You can't move on to the next stage of setting up your author website until DNS updates most of the world's Internet address book to include your new site. It can take up to 48 hours, but this is rare. It will take several hours to make any progress, though.

You need to wait at least two hours, although my recommendation is that you come back and complete the next section tomorrow; which makes this the perfect point for you to stop and do some writing.

Chapter 10
Your Author Website: Set up WordPress

In this chapter, we're completing the second stage of your author website setup—setting up WordPress.

Add Domain

1. First, go to the Website/SSL page on your WPX dashboard. Click **Add New Website**. Enter the author domain name you registered in the last chapter. Click **Create Website**. It will take a minute or two, but when it's complete, WPX shows a success message (screenshot on next page).

2. Next, add a security certificate and SSL to your website. Security certificates are no longer optional for websites. Google will not rank your site if it isn't secure. Click on the green **SSL** button next to your new domain name and select "Install Free Certificate". This will take a minute or two to install; you will get a message when it's complete.

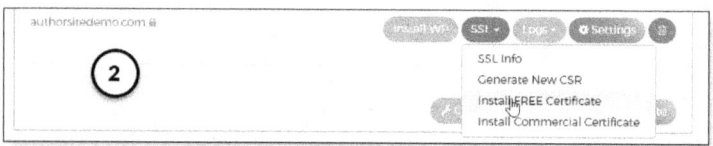

Install WordPress

3. Now you need to install WordPress. Click on the blue **Install WP** button next to your domain name and then click the "Install WordPress on Website" link.

- Make sure the admin email is correct. You can add a new admin user name, or accept the default.

- Add an admin password and check the "IGNORE EXISTING WORDPRESS INSTALL (IF ANY)" checkbox. Click the big green **Deploy WordPress** button.

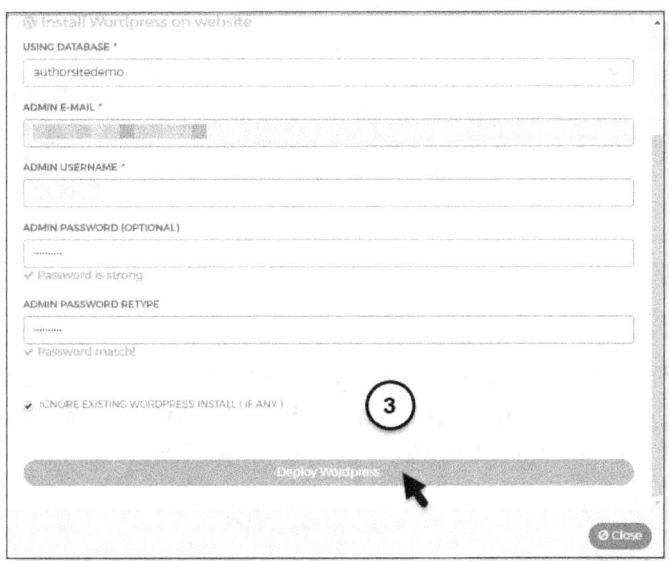

As with the other install steps, this will take a minute or two and display a success message with your admin login and password. Write these down somewhere secure in case you forget them.

4. Back on the WPX dashboard, you can now click on your author domain name, and your new WordPress site will show in the browser.

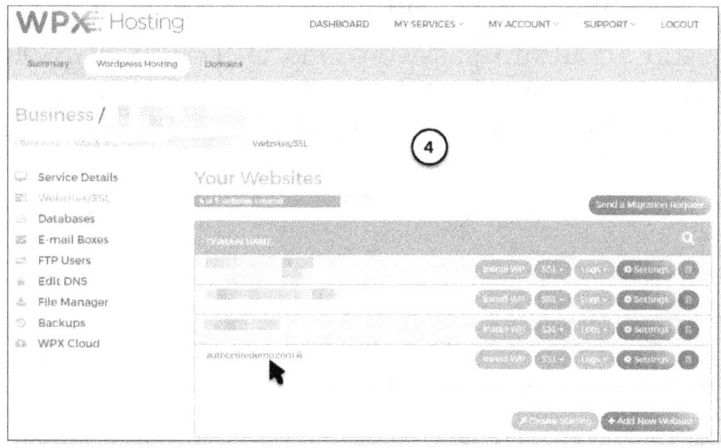

5. Scroll down the page and click **Log In** under the "Meta" title. Enter the admin username and password to log in to the WordPress dashboard.

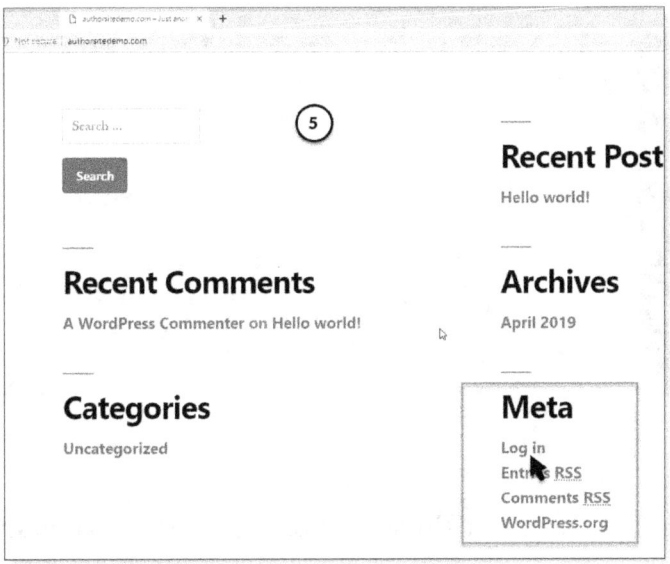

Set Up WordPress

Once you log in to your WordPress site, your WordPress dashboard displays.

As you can see, the WordPress dashboard is quite busy. If you're non-technical, you might feel somewhat uncomfortable right now. There is no need to be overwhelmed though as you will only use a small part of WordPress regularly.

It's one of the few gripes I have with WordPress—because it tries to be everything to everybody, it has lots of extra stuff most of us will never use.

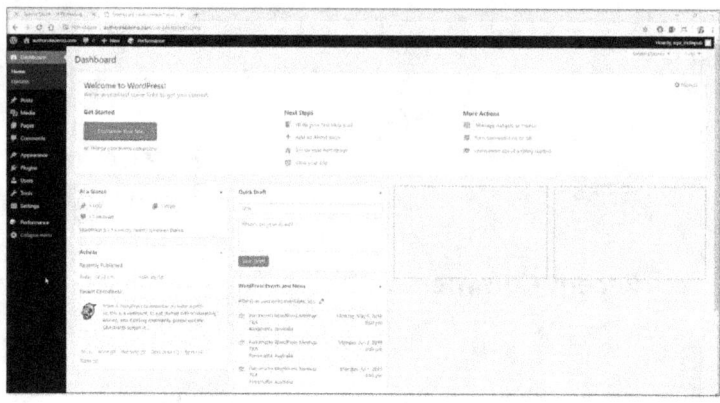

To finish the WordPress setup, we need to complete 3 tasks:

 i. Add a plugin for a contact form and a plugin for SSL security
 ii. Add some draft pages (You'll add the content in Chapter 10); and
 iii. Create the menu for the site.

We also need to change some settings as we go along. None of these tasks are difficult, and the whole process should not take more than an hour.

Once these tasks are complete, the only parts of WordPress, you will need to interact with are:

- **Posts**—where you add blog content, new stories and news; and

- **Pages**—which you only update when you have new books or need to edit your profile.

  6. To start, we will change some settings. Click on **Settings** in the left menu, and then select **General**.

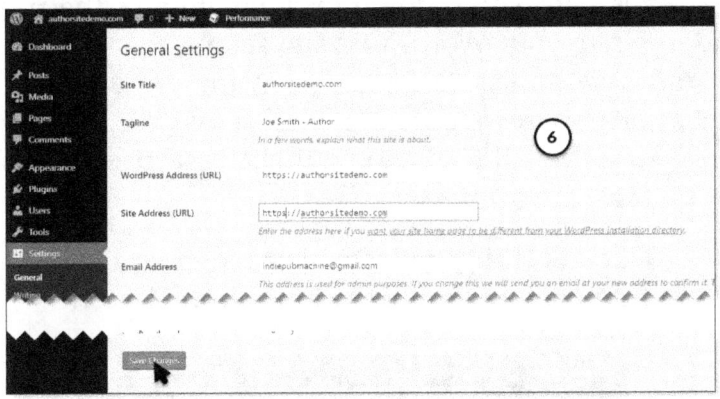

- Change the tagline to "[Your Name] - Author". You can change the tagline to whatever you want, but this is a common default.

- Next, change the WordPress Address and Site Address from HTTP to HTTPS. The "S" on the end makes your URL secure—any traffic directed to your site will now use the security certificate you installed.

- Scroll down and click **Save Changes**.

At this point, your site will break and show a big scary message. This is because you logged in on an insecure HTTP link and have set your site to use only secure HTTPS links.

This is normal—close the browser window and go back to your WPX dashboard.

Click your new domain name again to reopen your WordPress site, scroll down to the bottom of the page, and log in to your WordPress site again.

You may still get security warning messages, but that's OK—we're about to install a plugin that will make sure that all traffic to your site is secure and you get no more warnings.

7. Click on **Plugins** in the left menu and click the **Add New** button at the top of your screen.

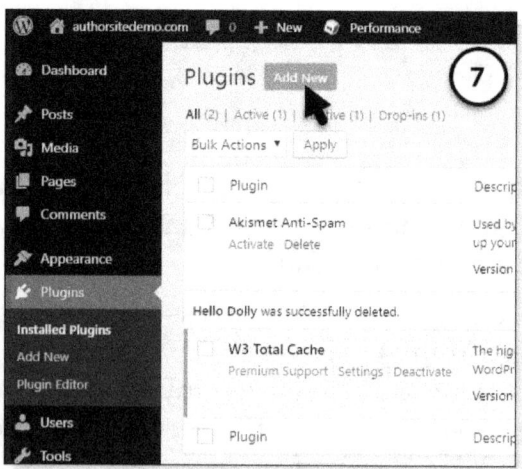

- Search for "Really Simple SSL"

- When the Really Simple SSL tile appears, click the **Install Now button**. Once it is installed, click **Activate** to activate the plugin.

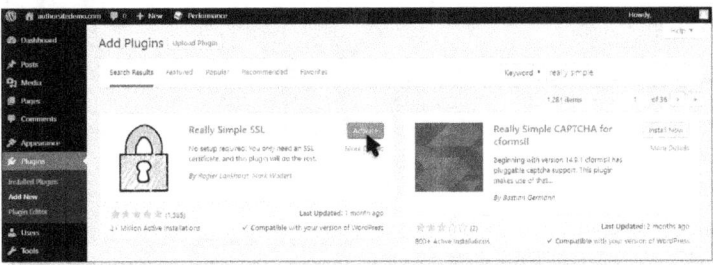

When the next screen opens, activate SSL by clicking the **Go ahead, activate SSL** button. It's safe to ignore the messages—your site is new, and none of these recommendations apply.

- While we're still in plugins, we will add a plugin for your contact form. Click **Add New**.
- Search for "WPForms" and install the "Contact Form by WPForms" plugin.
- Activate the plugin and the WPForms setup screen opens (screenshot on next page).

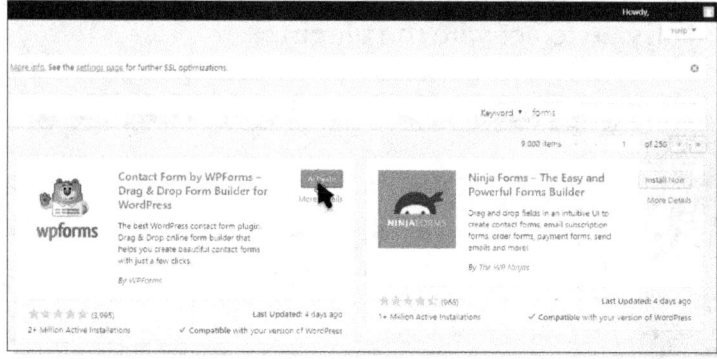

- Click **Create Your First Form**.

- Click **Create a Simple Contact Form**.

- Click on the form title in the edit screen and change Form Name to "Contact Us".
- Click **SAVE** in the top right of your browser.

- Click on **EMBED** to show the shortcode for the form. Don't worry too much about what shortcodes are right now—they're a special script that will embed something in a WordPress page or post.

You need to copy the shortcode and save it somewhere safe—you will need it soon.

Once you have copied the shortcode, close the pop-up and close the form window to go back to the WordPress dashboard.

8. Now we have a couple more settings to change. Click on **Settings->Discussion**. We will turn off user comments on your author website. WordPress' native comments are an open invitation for trolls and endless spam messages. It's far better to keep your reader communications either by email or in your social media groups.

Make sure the first three checkboxes are unchecked like in the screenshot.

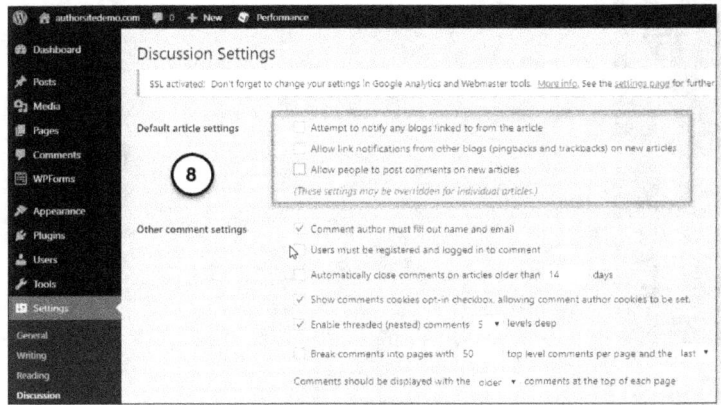

- When you've finished, scroll down and click **Save Changes**.

- Now click **Permalinks** and check that the permalink is set to "Post name". This is the default in WordPress 5, but it helps to check because permalinks are difficult to change later (screenshot on next page).

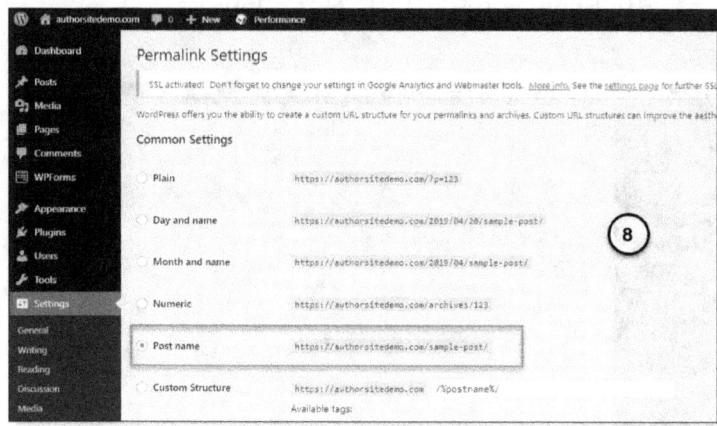

- If you have to change the setting, make sure you click **Save Changes**.

Add Pages

Now we will add some pages to your site. In this chapter, we will only add the page titles and placeholder content. We will add the content in the next chapter.

The reason we add placeholders first is so we can set up a menu. You can't create a menu without having pages to assign to each menu item.

9. Click on **Pages->Add New**.

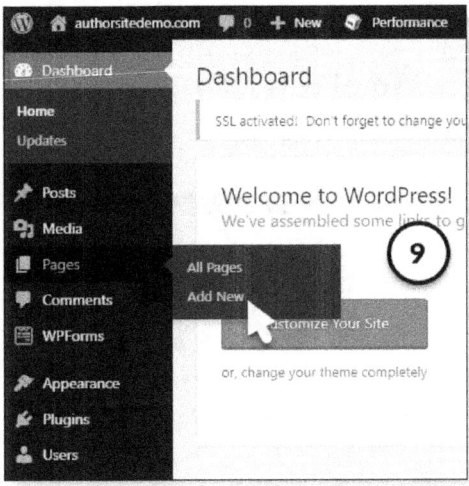

- Enter "Home" as the title. Add some placeholder text in the page body. Click **Publish**.

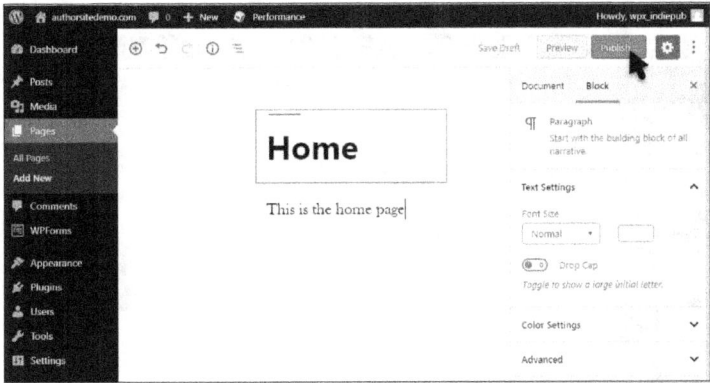

- Create another new page. Enter "Blog" as the title. You don't have to enter any placeholder text for this page—WordPress manages blog pages for you. Click **Publish**.

- Repeat this process to create an "About" page. Click **Publish**.

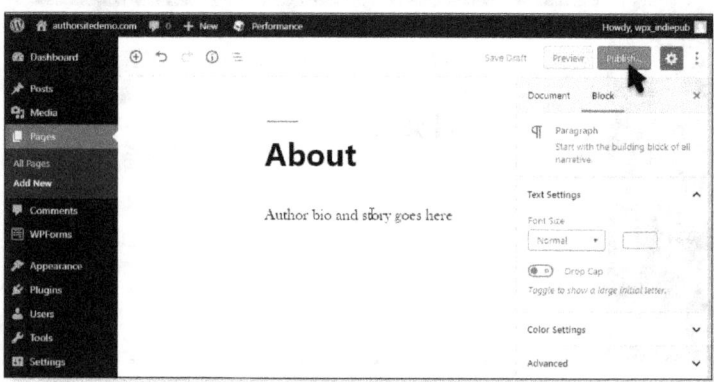

- Finally, create your "Contact" page. Once you have added some intro text, click on the plus icon (⊕) and select "Shortcode" to add the contact form to the page. Shortcodes are under the widgets category. This is where that shortcode you saved a little while ago goes.

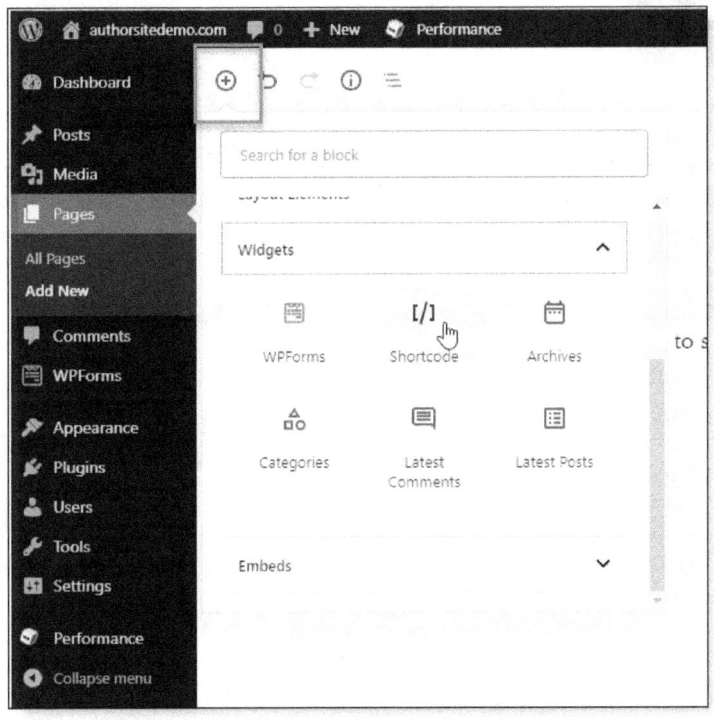

- Select the shortcode widget and paste the shortcode you copied. Click **Publish** (screenshot on next page).

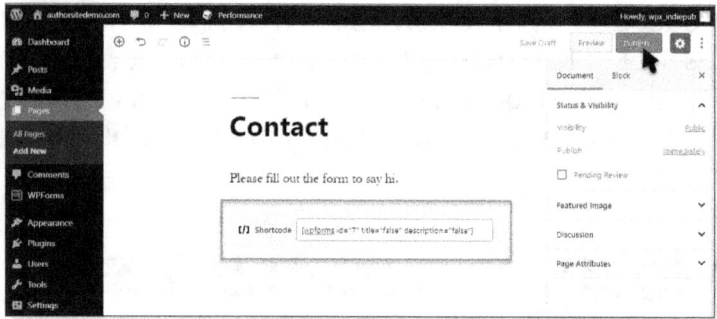

To test out if your new form works, click **Preview**. Your browser should display the contact form the plugin created for you.

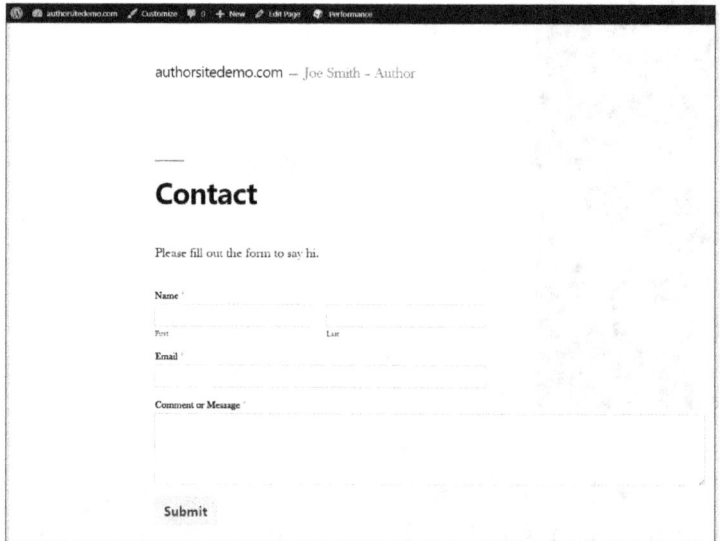

Set up Menu and Navigation

10. Go back to the dashboard and select **Settings-> Reading**.

- Set "Your homepage displays" to "A static page". Set "Home" as your homepage, and "Blog" as your posts page.
- Click **Save Changes**.

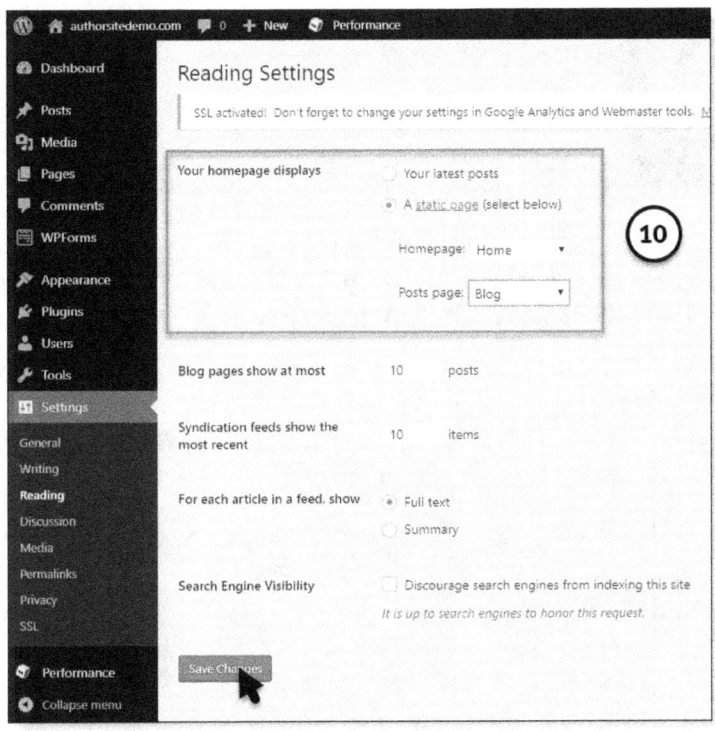

11. Click **Appearance->Menus**.

- Enter "Top Menu" in the menu name text box and click create menu.

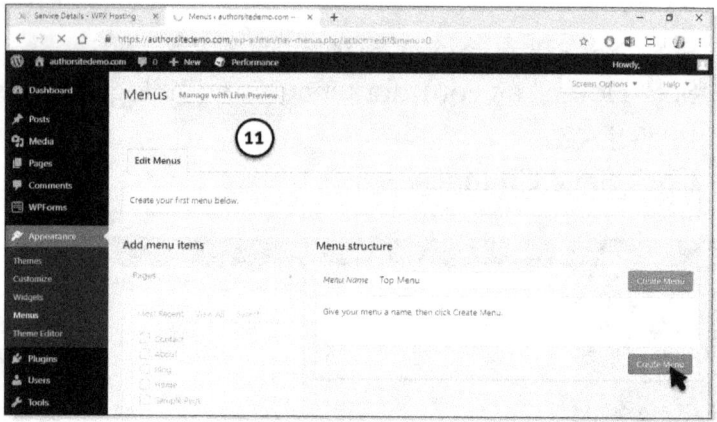

- Now check the four pages you just created in the "Pages" tile and click **Add to Menu**.

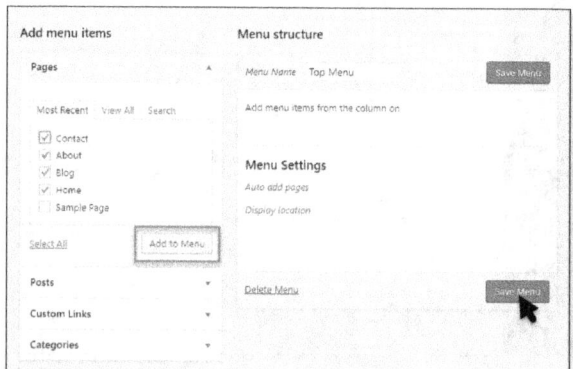

- You can rearrange the menu items to suit your tastes. I'm arranging them into a standard layout. Click **Save Menu** when you are finished.

12. To add the new menu to your site, click on **Appearance** again, but this time click on **Customize**. On the customization menu, click **Menus** (screenshot on next page).

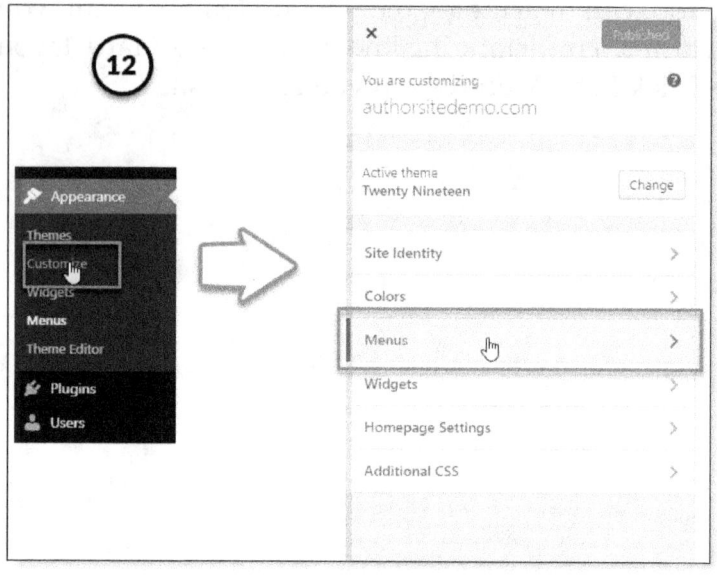

- Select "Top Menu".

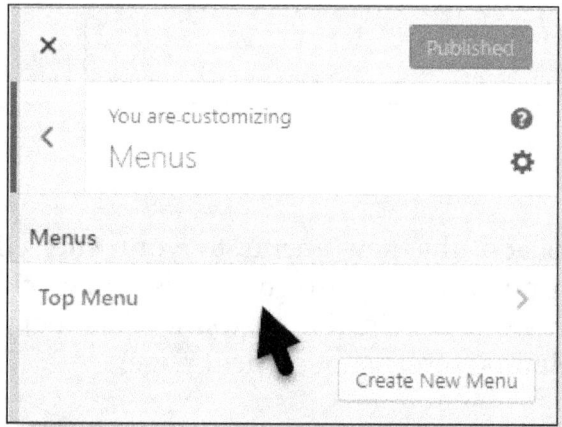

- Check the "Primary" checkbox. Click **Publish** and close the customization menu.

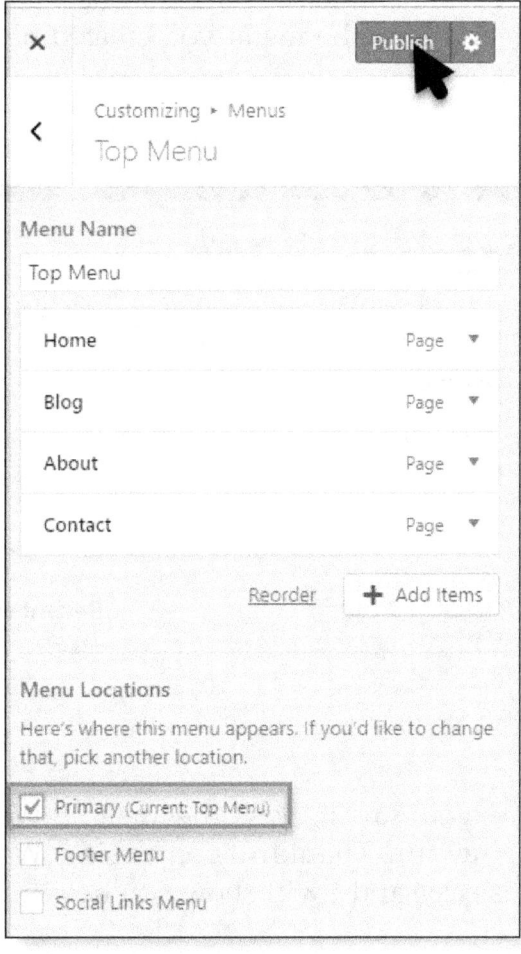

Now, if you click the home icon in the top left of your browser, the configured site will display. Take some time to explore the home page. Try each of the menu items in the top menu to see how your new pages fit in the layout, and how the menu you created helps with navigation.

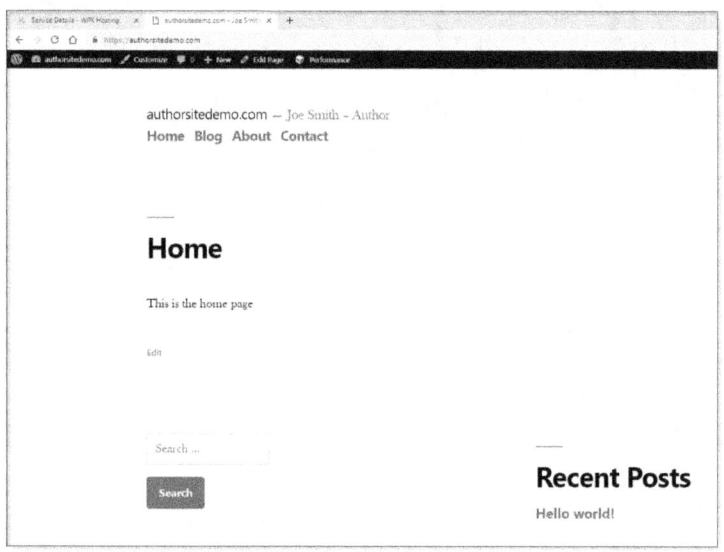

And before you say it, yes, the default WordPress template is awful. Thankfully, changing WordPress templates is easy, and I will show you how in the next chapter.

The reason we don't fiddle with templates now is that you can't see how a template works with your content until you have a decent amount of content on the site.

Playing with templates can also be an enormous time sink, so it's much better to get the content sorted before Creative Brain takes over and you spend 7 hours testing out color schemes.

That's it for this chapter. Most of the boring *tick this, check that, install the other* process is complete now—in the next chapter we will write some content to replace the placeholders we created.

Chapter 11
Your Author Website: Content

In this chapter, we will add content to the pages we created in the last chapter.

We've covered this earlier, but for review—the minimum you need for an effective author website is:

1. A list of your current and upcoming books
2. An author bio
3. Free outreach content
4. Calls to action aimed at increasing the size of your mailing list; and
5. An easy means of contacting you

We've already completed the last task—we created the contact form and contact page in Chapter 10.

Add Your Books

If you have more than two or three books, you should create a separate page for them, but as we'll only add two books in this demo, I will put them on the home page of the site.

1. Starting from the WordPress dashboard, click on **Pages**. Click on the "Home" title to open the home page for editing.

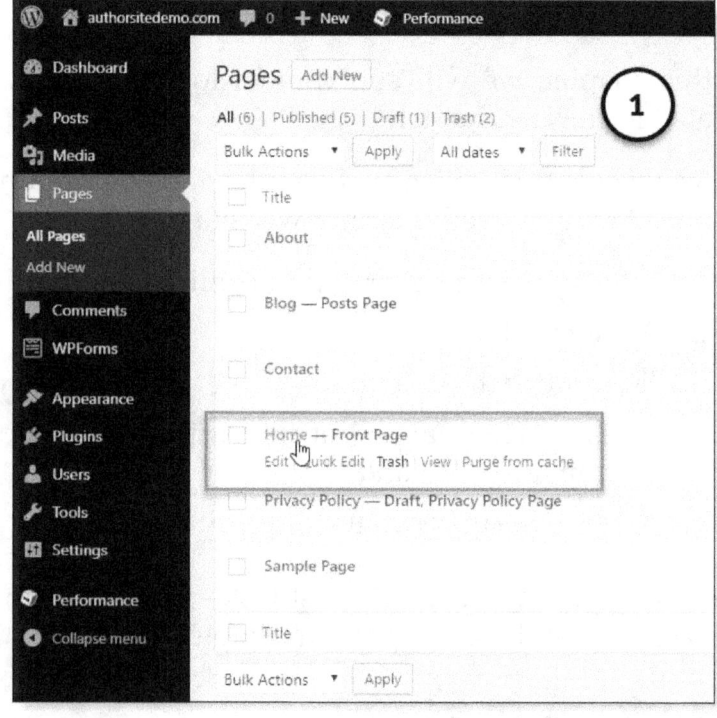

- First, I'm adding a simple intro and linking it to the About page.

Home

Joe Smith is an awesome author who has won millions of awards. Read more.

- Next, we're adding some books to the home page. As we will have book cover images with text to the side, the best way to lay this out is with columns. Click on the plus icon (⊕) and add a column block; the block defaults to two columns, which is what we want (screenshot on next page).

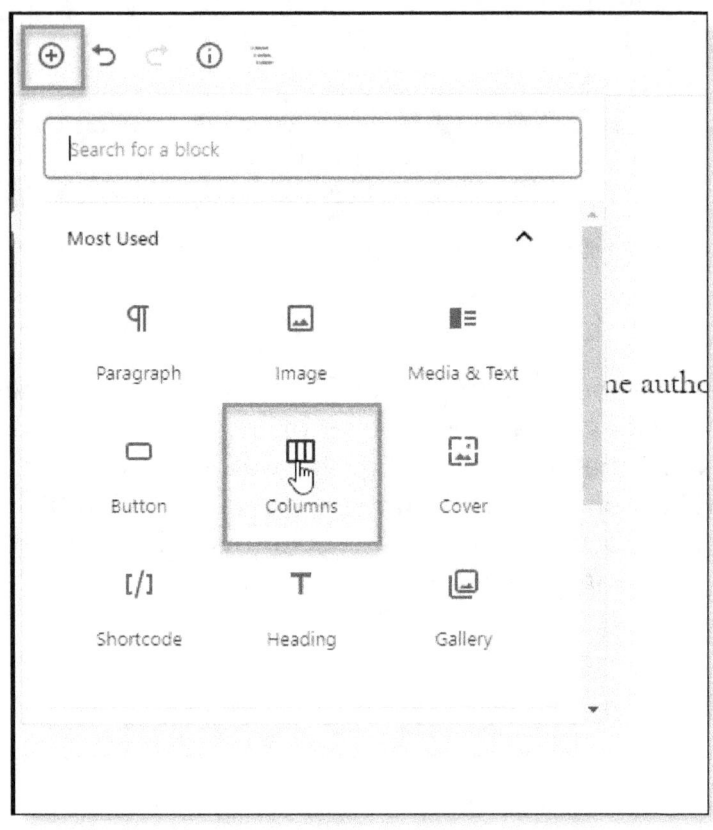

- Make sure the cursor is in the left column, and add an image block. I will upload the cover image from my computer.

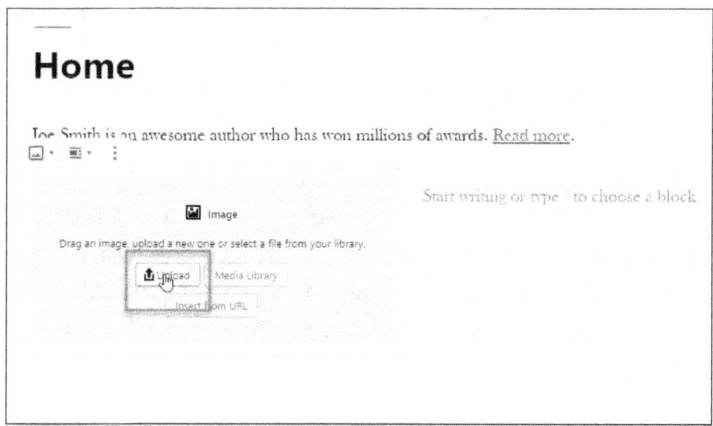

- Click in the right column and add the book blurb. This is a published book, so we'll add a button that takes the site visitor to the book's Amazon page. You don't have a book to link to right now, so enter a pound sign (#) in the button link.

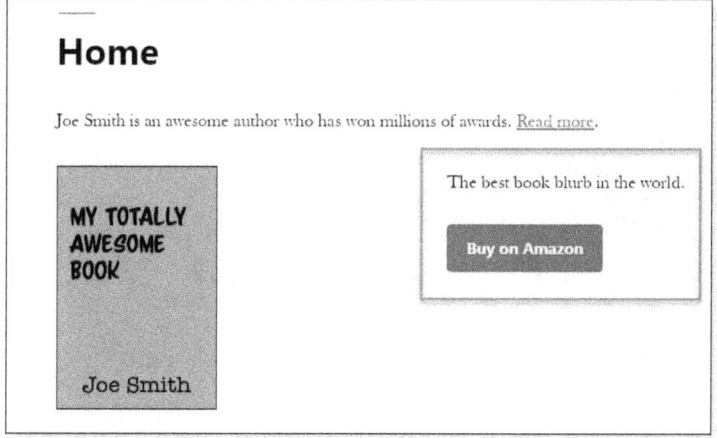

- Repeat this process to add an upcoming book. Click on the plus icon to add a column block; Add an image block to the left column, upload a book cover, and enter a book blurb.

As this is an upcoming book, we want to collect email addresses from readers who want to join the waiting list for the book. We will add the MailChimp form later in the chapter. For the moment, we're adding some placeholder text to remind us to add the form.

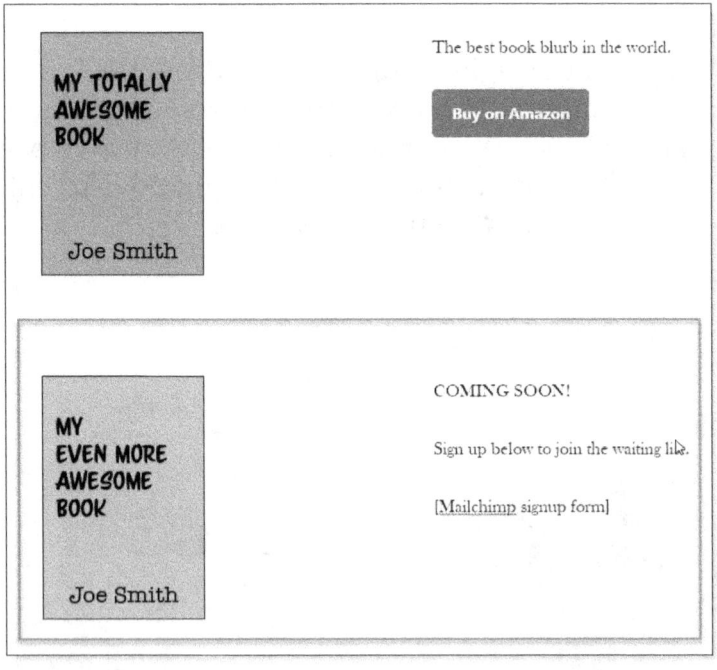

AUTHOR WEBSITE - ADD CONTENT 171

- Finally, we'll add a short message and a placeholder for the newsletter sign-up form. We will add this form later in the chapter. Add a content block below the upcoming book, and add a message and placeholder text for the form.

- Click on **Update** to save the changes.
- If you click **Preview** on the top right of your browser, you can see how the updated home page looks to site visitors.

Update the About Page

Now we'll add content to the About page.

About pages can be as long or as short as you like, but they should at least have a short bio and your author photo, which we're adding now.

2. We'll use the same two-column layout we used on the home page, so add a column block above the existing text block.

- Drag the author bio block into the left column
- Now add an image to the right column

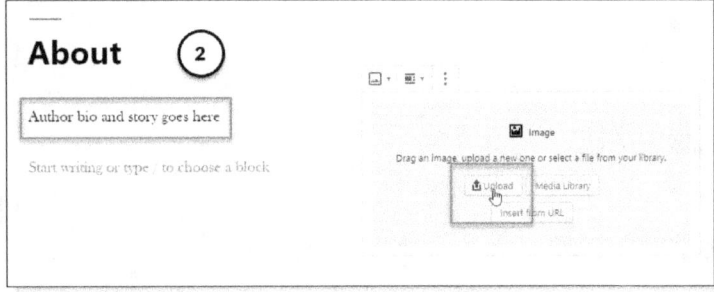

Preview the page to see if you're happy with the results; then update the page.

Add Posts (Outreach)

The difference between posts and pages in WordPress is you add and update posts periodically, whereas pages are static and don't change often.

Posts are where you publish outreach content for your website.

While WordPress defaults to calling your posts a blog, it doesn't have to be a blog. Your posts can be any outreach content you wish.

You can serialize new stories, blog a whole book, diarize your writing journey, review favorite books—anything you enjoy doing, and provides greater engagement with your readers is excellent.

You can also do nothing if you don't have time. Remember WIBBOW? and remember that marketing time can't exceed writing time.

If you don't want to publish content on your site now, remove the blog link from your menu. Don't delete the page as you might change your mind later; removing it from the menu makes it invisible on your site.

If you keep the blog and intend to post content periodically—remember the most important thing: to be outreach, your content must encourage readers to join your mailing list.

Each piece of content must have a Call To Action attached; even if it's only a newsletter sign-up box at the bottom of each post.

3. To add a post, click on "Posts" in the left menu, then click the **Add New** button.

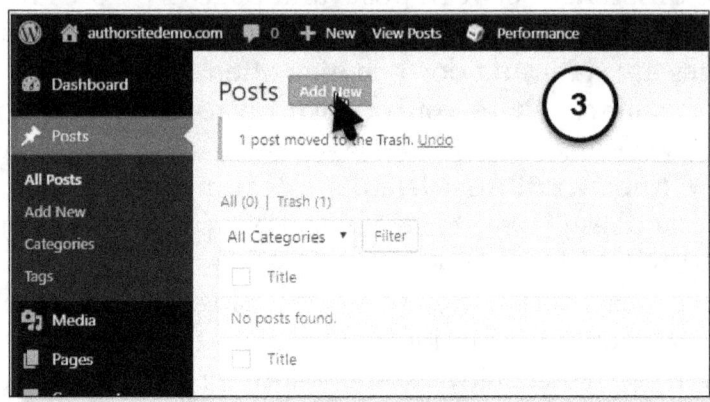

Creating a blog post is as easy as giving the piece a title and adding content. The WordPress editor is a powerful tool, so take the time to learn the different content blocks you can add to a post.

I will leave it for you to decide what your first piece of outreach content will be. Remember to click **Publish** when you're finished!

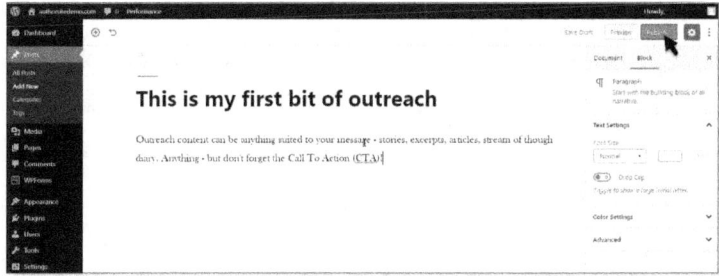

Change the Sidebar Content

Now it's time to change your sidebar content.

Click on the home icon at the top of your browser to open your website. If you scroll down to the bottom of the page, you will see the widgets added by WordPress (Comments, Categories, Meta, etc.). Screenshot on next page.

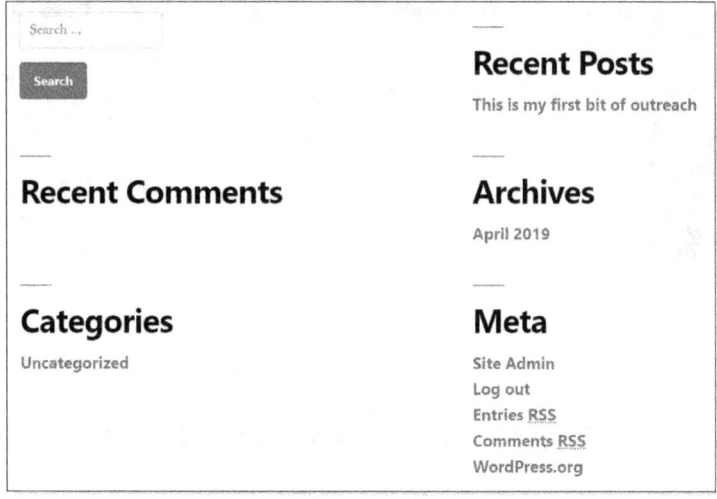

While it might not be evident in the rather pedestrian default template, these widgets show up in the sidebar of higher quality templates.

The sidebar is a great place to add a sign-up form as it shows on every page on the site.

    4. Click on "Customize" on the top toolbar. Select "Widgets".

- First, we'll get rid of the widgets we don't want to show in the sidebar. Click on the down arrow next to "Meta" and click **Remove**. Repeat for "Categories" and "Recent Comments".

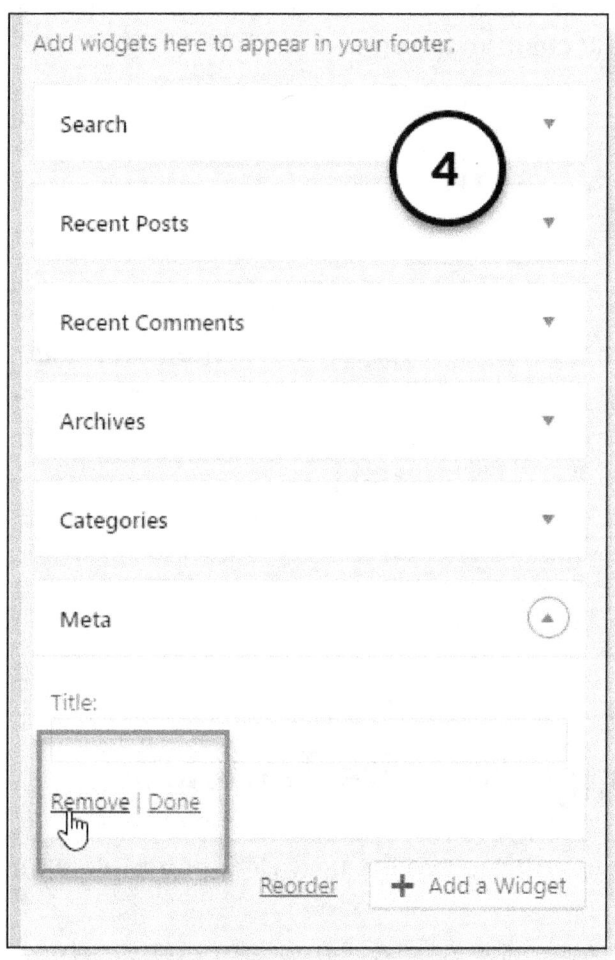

When you finish, you will only have "Search", "Recent Posts" and "Archives" in the list.

If you scroll to the bottom of the page, you can see that the widgets have been removed. Click **Publish** and close the customization menu.

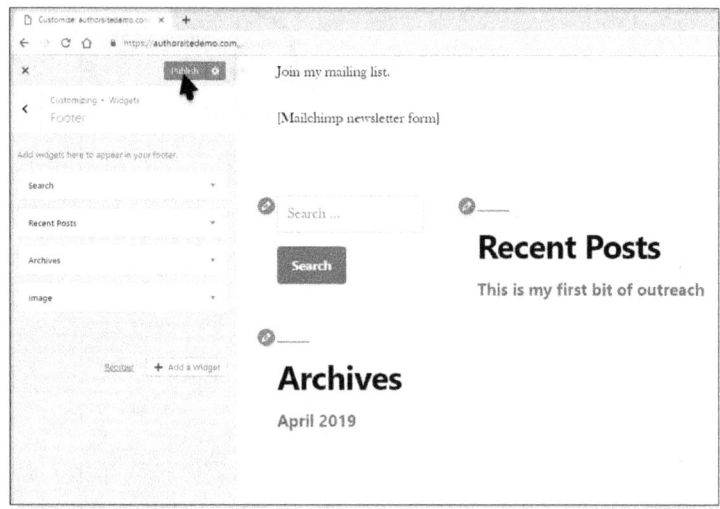

Change the Site Template

Next, we will replace the ugly default template for your site.

    5. Go back to the WordPress dashboard and select "Themes" from the "Appearance" menu.

Author Website - Add Content

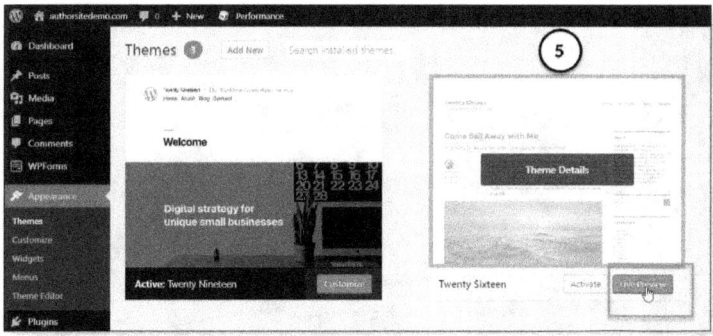

WordPress comes with a few themes already installed. To get an idea of how a theme changes your site's appearance, go over to the Twenty Sixteen theme and click the **Live Preview** button.

You can see that, while the new theme is still sparse, the layout has changed completely. Themes are one of WordPress' superpowers because, with little effort, you can make major changes to the look of your site.

And because WordPress is so popular, you also get many thousands of theme designs to choose from in the WordPress marketplace. Close the customize window and click on **Add New Theme** to see what I mean (screenshot on next page).

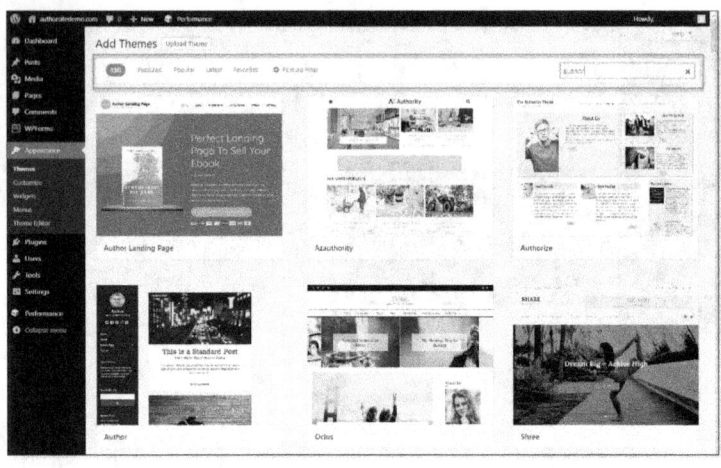

This is only a sample of the themes available. WordPress only shows themes from the WordPress marketplace—many thousands more are available in other marketplaces. If you search "WordPress theme" in your favorite browser, you will see what I mean.

You can filter templates by "Featured", "Popular" and "Latest". You can also search for themes using keywords.

If you hover over any of the theme tiles, you can preview the theme. If you want to try out the theme with your content, you can install it.

As this is not a WordPress tutorial, I won't go into detail on how to install and configure themes. It would be a waste of your time and my time anyway, as you are certain to have different ideas about how your author site should look.

Now you have added the basic content, I encourage you to let Creative Brain loose and play with the themes for a while. Don't be surprised if you lose track of a few hours because I do every time.

Remember, as long as you don't delete or change content, you can't break anything right now. If you wreck a theme by changing colors or mess with the formatting, switch to another theme. If you want to use the theme you broke, uninstall and reinstall the theme to reset all the settings.

For the rest of the book, I will use the Twenty Sixteen template. It's plain, and I wouldn't use it on a real website, but at least it's not as awful as the default.

Now it's time to integrate some MailChimp forms into the site so that we can collect email addresses from our readers.

Add MailChimp Forms

First, we'll configure the main audience list MailChimp set up for you when you created the account. You must log in to MailChimp to complete the following.

1. From the MailChimp dashboard, click on "Audience" in the top menu and select "View Audiences" from the Manage Audiences drop-down (screenshot on next page).

- MailChimp will automatically name your main subscriber list after the account name. Click on the list name.

- Click on "Settings" and select "Audience name and defaults".

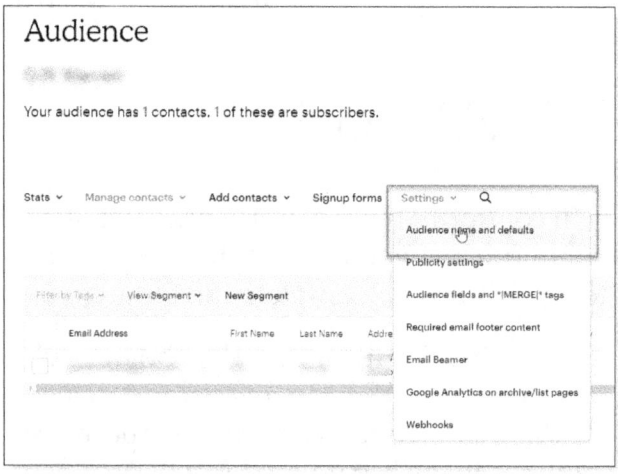

- Change the audience name to something more descriptive. I am naming it "Main Audience".
- You can also change other list settings on this page. For example, you can change the default display name and email for when you send messages and newsletters to your subscribers. As you can change these settings at the message level, I leave them alone.
- The one thing you do want to update on this page is the New Subscriber Notifications. Add email addresses to each notification you want to receive. I only want a daily digest so I will put the account email address in here.
- Save the settings.

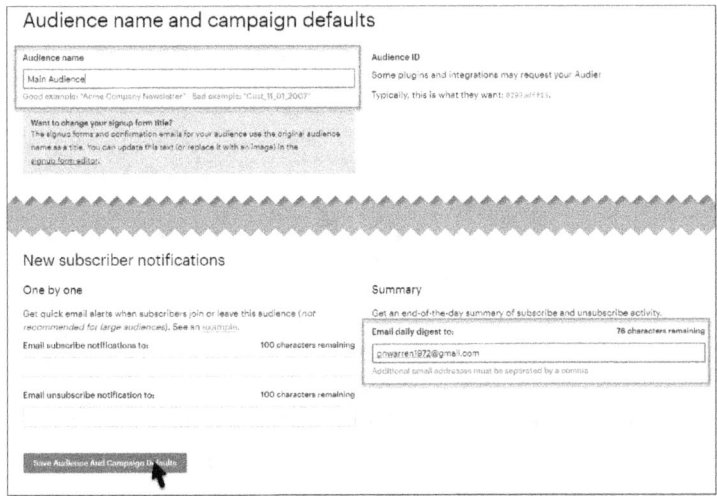

2. Now we need to create the form for our website. From the MailChimp dashboard, click the **Create** button on the top right of your browser.

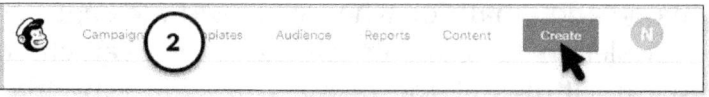

- Select "Sign-up Form" from the pop-up dialog box. Click **Begin**.

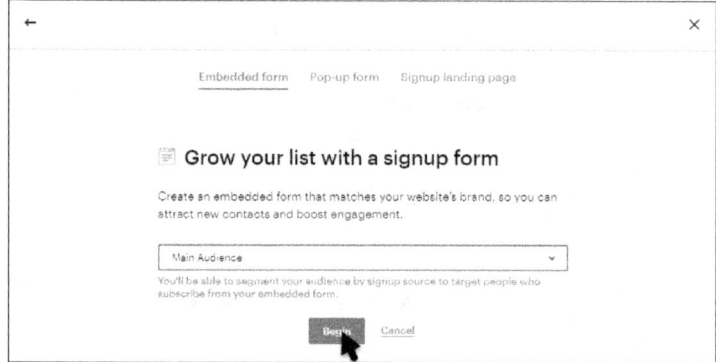

- There are several form designs to choose from. I will use the Horizontal layout for this form.
- Change the form title to something that suits your newsletter. When you hit enter, MailChimp will auto-generate the form code for you.

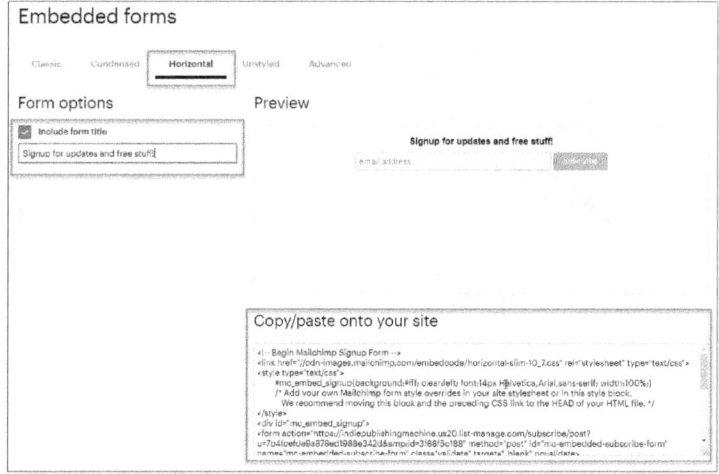

- Copy the code and switch back to your website dashboard.
- Select your home page and scroll down to the form placeholder you added in the last chapter.
- Switch to "Edit as HTML". Replace the placeholder text by pasting the code you copied from MailChimp (screenshot on next page).

If you click **Preview**, you can see how the new form looks on your site. Once you update your home page, the form will display each time a user visits the page. Easy as that.

3. Next, we'll create the waiting list form for an upcoming book (screenshot on next page).

- Go back to the MailChimp dashboard and create another sign-up form.
- We will use the Condensed form style this time. Enter a suitable title and copy the code.

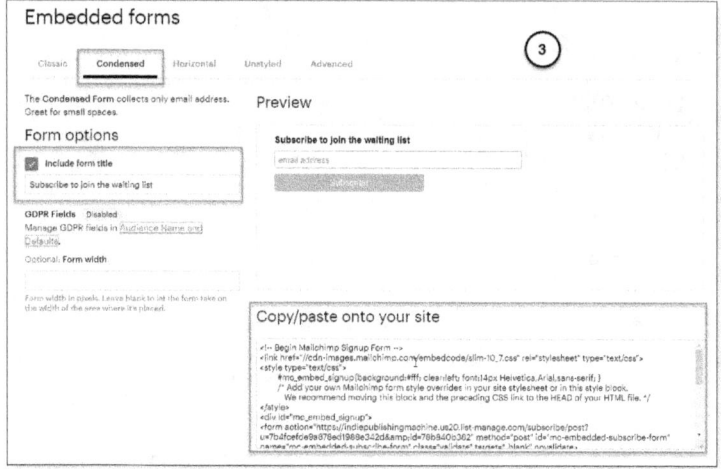

- Switch back to the home page and replace the placeholder text next to the upcoming book with the form code. As the form has a title asking visitors to subscribe, I will change the introductory text to a book blurb. It's up to you what you put in here though.

- Click on **Update** to update the page. If you view the page now, you can see the new waiting list form is showing on the page.

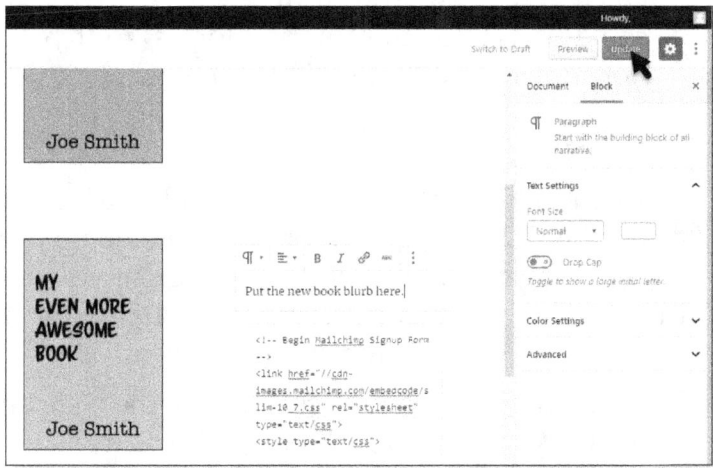

Note the waiting list form and the newsletter form link to the same audience in MailChimp. This is a limitation of MailChimp's free account.

There isn't a simple way to tell whether someone signed up for the newsletter or signed up for the waiting list.

When you think about it, this is not a problem. You will email everyone on your list when your new book is available, even if the subscriber is not on the waiting list.

Before we finish, I'll show you how to add one more form to the site—a form that displays at the end of a blog post.

4. Jump back to the MailChimp dashboard, and create a new sign-up form. We're following the same process as the last two forms, so if you're not sure, check the previous screenshots.

- Click **Begin**.
- Select the Horizontal form style and enter a title for the form. Like the two forms on the home page, we're adding subscribers to a single list, so you can't differentiate between sign-ups, but while your list is small, this won't be much of a problem.
- Once you have created the form, copy the code and switch back to your WordPress dashboard.

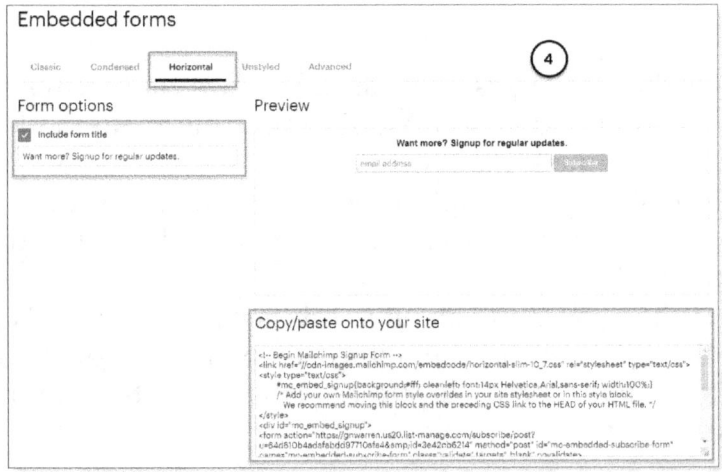

- Open up the blog post you created the last chapter.

- Click on the paragraph block. In a real article or blog post, this will be the last paragraph in the post.
- Click on the More Options icon and select "Edit as HTML".
- Below the existing HTML code, paste the form code.

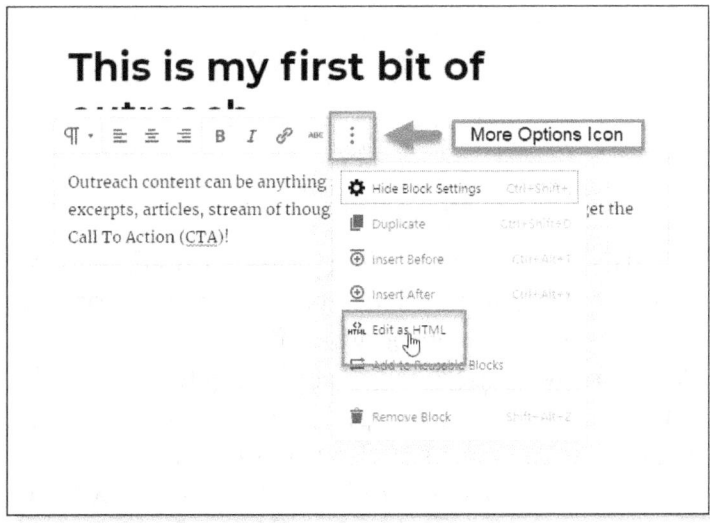

- Click **Preview** to see how the form looks, and if you're happy with the form, update the page (screenshot on next page).

Follow this same process every time you add outreach content to your site to ensure each item you post has a Call to Action (CTA) embedded into it.

You can get much more sophisticated with CTAs in your content. For example, you can provide a PDF copy of your article as a download. However, this is a paid option, and I wanted to start you off with free options, so you can build your list without worrying about paying for subscriptions.

That's it for adding MailChimp forms to your website. If you search around, you will find many plugins that make adding MailChimp forms to a WordPress site easier; however, you must pay for the good quality ones.

The purpose of this section was to show you how to use MailChimp forms without having to pay for a plugin. If you want to explore your options, search

"MailChimp" in the WordPress plugin gallery. You can access the gallery by clicking **Plugins->Add New**.

We're finished adding content and forms to your site. It's also the end of the chapters on setting up your author website. Your author website is the most challenging thing you need to create, so congratulations on getting this far!

In the next chapter, I will show you how to publish your books on Amazon.

Chapter 12
Publish a Book on Amazon

In this chapter, I will show you how to publish your books on Amazon.

To publish books on Amazon, you need to set up a KDP account. KDP stands for Kindle Direct Publishing, which in the early days, was where independent authors could self-publish direct to the Kindle platform.

Now that CreateSpace and Kindle have merged, KDP is your all-in-one platform for publishing eBooks for Kindle and publishing paperbacks on Amazon and for distribution to bookstores.

Set up KDP Account

To set up your KDP account, go to the KDP website. You can search for "KDP" or enter "https://kdp.com" in the address bar of your browser.

You have two options when creating a KDP account:

1. Use your existing Amazon account; or
2. Create a new one for KDP.

It's up to you which way you go—if you create a new KDP account, you can keep everything related to your writing business separate to your personal stuff. But you might not want two Amazon logins, so in this case, it would be better for you to use your Amazon account.

I have always regretted not setting up a separate account because when you are in the business of being a writer, a lot of your Amazon purchases are tax deductible. It's a pain keeping legitimate business expenses separate from personal purchases when they're all in the same account. Every country is different, and you will have different needs, so your experience may be different from mine.

So you can see the complete process, I will set up a new account:

1. Enter your name, email, and a password and KDP will send a verification code to your email. Once you verify the code and accept the terms and conditions, your KDP dashboard will open in your browser.

kindle direct publishing

Create account

Your name

Indie Publishing

Email

indiepubmachine@gmail.com

Password

••••••••••

i Passwords must be at least 6 characters.

Re-enter password

••••••••••

Create your KDP account

By creating an account, you agree to Amazon's Conditions of Use and Privacy Notice.

Already have an account? Sign in ›

2. Before you can publish a book, you must enter additional account information. Click on "Update Now" at the top of your dashboard.

- Enter your address, contact information and your bank account details. Depending on which country you are in, Amazon pays either into your bank account by electronic funds transfer, or by wire transfer.

  Amazon has country-specific arrangements and restrictions for payments, so you must check the rules for your country; I can't give you any specific advice.

- Finally, you need to complete the tax interview. The tax interview determines how much tax Amazon will withhold from your royalties on behalf of the IRS. This is another thing I can't advise you on, but in broad terms, the tax Amazon deducts from your payments varies from country to country. You need to complete the tax interview to ensure Amazon deducts the right amount of tax.

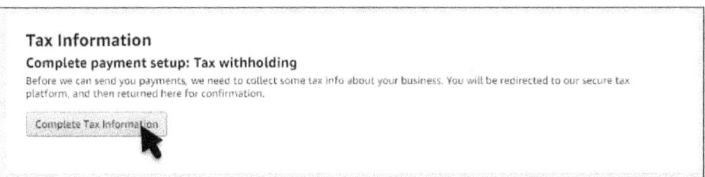

Once you have finished entering your banking and tax information, the warning at the top of your dashboard will disappear, and you will be ready to publish your books.

Add a Book

I assume that you have an eBook file formatted for Kindle, and you have a cover design ready to upload. If you don't, you need to have them ready before continuing.

3. First, log in to your KDP account and click on the create a Kindle eBook icon. The process for creating eBooks and paperbacks is the same, so I will only show you how to publish an eBook in this chapter.

- Enter your book title and author name.

- Enter a book description. This is often the same as your back cover blurb but can be anything that describes your book. Just remember the book description is one of the critical elements that will help your book sell, so if you are not good at copywriting, you need to hire a professional to do this for you.

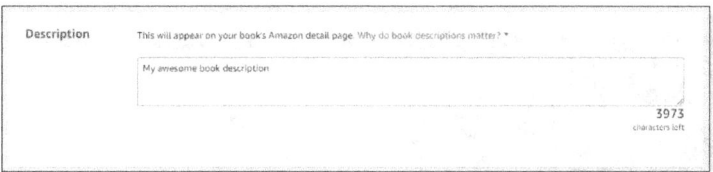

- Click the **I own the copyright...** button.

Keywords and Categories

Next, we need to select keywords and Amazon categories for your book.

While Amazon says keywords are optional, they're not—if you want your book to be searchable, you need keywords.

Amazon has some advice on picking keywords, but my favorite technique is to use Amazon's auto-suggest tool to help you find good keywords and keyphrases.

Let's say Joe Smith is ready to publish his latest cyberpunk dystopian romance. To find some useful keywords, go to Amazon's home page and start typing in a broad keyword. In this example, I'm entering "cyberpunk".

You can see from the screenshot that Amazon is suggesting search terms for you. The beauty of this technique is auto-suggest isn't making these terms up—these are actual search terms used by readers; listed in order of relative importance.

In this example, most people are searching for "Cyberpunk 2077" (which is a game, in case you're wondering) with Cyberpunk books coming in the top 10.

To get related keywords and phrases, you use a simple trick called the "alphabet soup" method. Type in your main keyword and then type the letter a:

In this screenshot, you can see "cyberpunk anthology" is a potential candidate for a keyphrase. Repeat the process with "cyberpunk b" and work your way through the alphabet to collect useful keywords and phrases.

You should complete this exercise with two or more primary keywords; for example, Joe could also use "dystopia" and "romance" as additional primary keywords.

Amazon allows up to seven keywords and phrases. Once you have a reasonable number of potential keywords and phrases, select seven of your favorites.

Don't throw out the rest of your list though—you can use these extra keywords and phrases later for other books in the same genre, or on your website for Search Engine Optimization (SEO).

Next, we need to find some categories for the book.

The best way to find book categories is to look at other books similar to yours. You can search for books if you know the title or author, or you can browse the best-seller lists for books like yours.

You can also do a broad search, which is what I'm doing in this example:

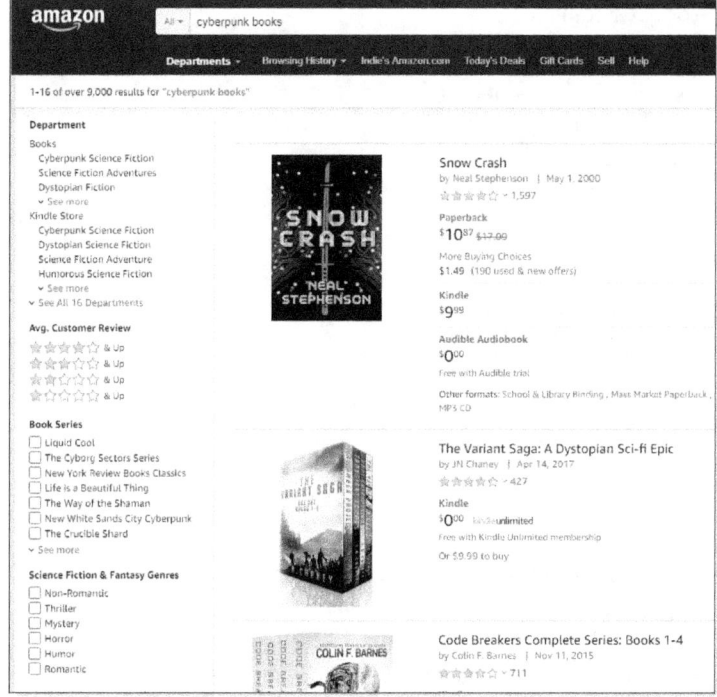

You can see from the screenshot I have searched for "cyberpunk books".

Whichever method you use, the book's categories are listed in the "Product Details" section on the book's page on Amazon (screenshot on next page).

Repeat the process until you have 3 or more categories you can use.

4. Switch back to your KDP account and add the keywords and phrases from your research.

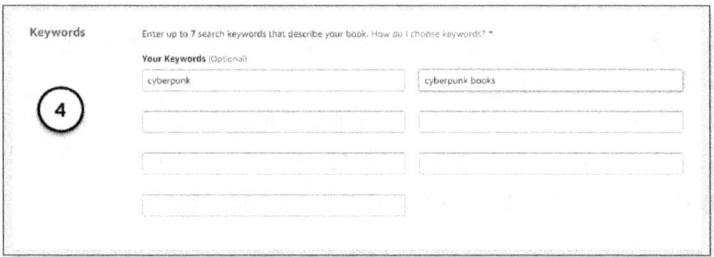

- Once you have added your keywords and key phrases, click the **Set Categories** button to search for categories that match the books you found in your research.

  Now comes the frustrating part. Not only will you find similar categories listed in multiple sections, but the categories often don't match with the categories you selected.

- The aim is to select a category that is as close as possible. Don't worry too much about picking the right categories first go as they're easy to change later. I am going to the "Fiction" category and selecting "Science Fiction > Genetic Engineering" as my first category and "Dystopian" as my second.

- You only get to pick two categories. Once they're selected, click **Save**.

- Moving down the form, you can select age and US grade ranges for your book, although I leave these alone.

- Once you've completed the form, click the **Save and Continue** button at the bottom of the page.

   5. At the top of the next page, select "No" to Digital Rights Management (DRM). Readers hate DRM and selecting "Yes" will kill your sales. As much as it sounds like a great idea, don't do it. Click the **Upload eBook Manuscript** button.

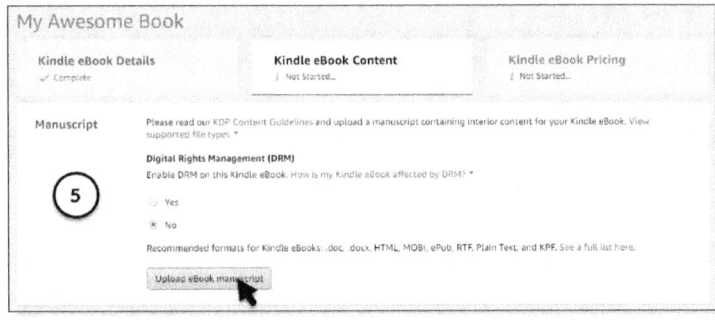

- Next, upload a cover file (JPEG or TIFF).

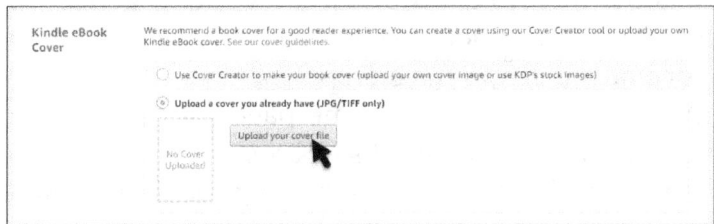

- Now you need to wait a while for Amazon to process the files. When Amazon finishes processing the files, you can open the Online Previewer.

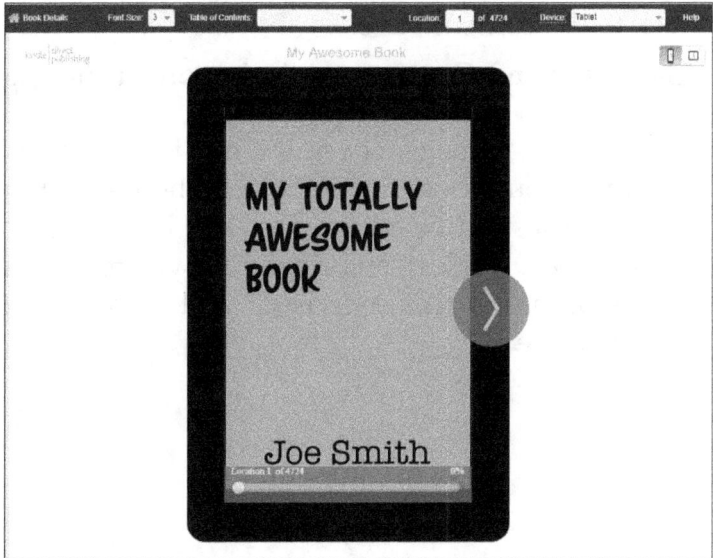

Check that the cover and content look as expected. This is the time to do yourself a favor and go through every page of the book to make sure it looks OK, and no formatting errors have crept in.

Make sure you check some pages at different font sizes to ensure reflow works OK too.

Be warned that eBook formatting for Kindle can be tricky, so don't be surprised if a few errors creep in at this stage. If you have formatting problems, make notes, and get screenshots so you can send the book back to whoever formatted it for you for them to correct the errors.

- Once you're happy with the preview, click **Book Details** in the top right of your browser to take you back to the content page.
- Click **Save and Continue** at the bottom of the page.

6. On the next page, check the box if you want to enroll your book in KDP Select. There are plenty of articles online on the pros and cons of enrolling in KDP Select, so I encourage you to do your research. For this exercise, I will leave the box unchecked.

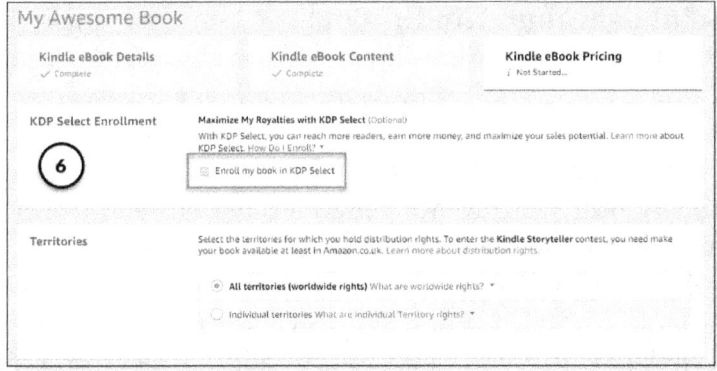

- Leave Territories alone and scroll down to set your pricing.
- For eBooks, always select 70% royalties. To qualify for 70% royalties, price your book between $2.99 and $9.99. I will enter $2.99. Amazon will give you an estimate of your book royalties per sale.

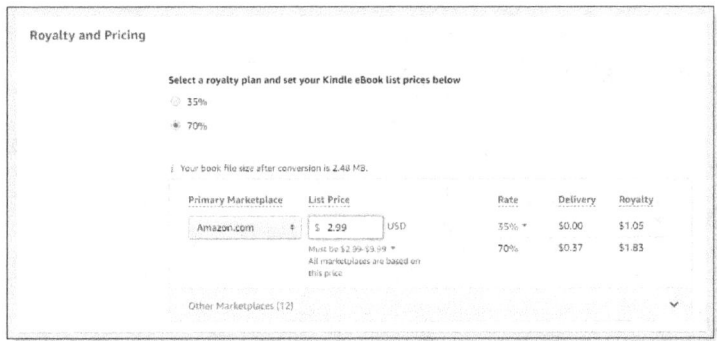

- Scroll down to the bottom of the page and click **Publish Your Kindle Book**. When you click the button, your book will publish, and you're ready to go.

Amazon says it takes up to 72 hours for a book to publish, but waiting more than a day before your book is up for sale on all Amazon's global sites is rare.

Amazon will send you an email once your book is available for sale. When you receive this email, there is one last thing you need to do—add a link from your author website to the published book.

Add a Book Link to Your Website

7. Go back to your KDP bookshelf. In the screenshot, I am in my non-fiction publishing account as a book must be available for sale for the next step to work.

- Hover over "View on Amazon" next to the book you just published and click "US".

- When Amazon opens your book page, copy the book URL from your browser's address bar.

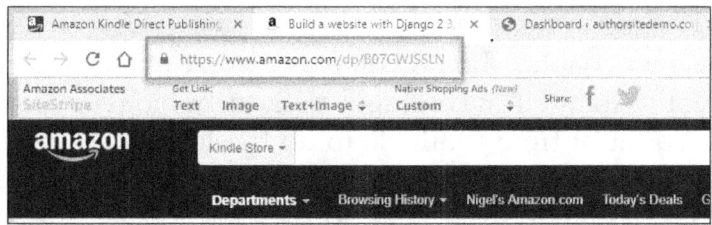

- Log in to your author website and open your home page for editing.
- Click the **Buy on Amazon** button. Paste the book URL into the button link. Make sure you delete the pound(#) sign. Click on the **Enter** icon.

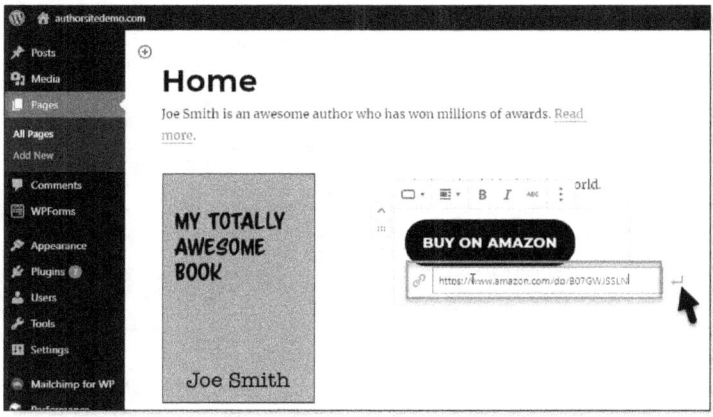

Once you update the page, when you click on the **Buy on Amazon** button, your new book page opens.

Well done! Now the book is published, all you have to do is write your next book :).

The next chapter should come as a great relief to those of you who are not confident with technology or don't have a lot of time available to do the technical bits. In the next chapter, I will show you how to find professional freelancers that will do the jobs you don't want to do.

Chapter 13
Getting Professional Help

If you are technically challenged, this chapter is for you.

If you are struggling to find a good editor, get a cover designed, or get a book formatted this chapter is for you.

And if you understand all the steps needed to set up your indie publishing business, but have said to yourself, *"I can do all of this, but you know what, I would rather write"*, this chapter is also for you.

For a new author, there is one relevant benefit to a traditional publisher. They will do all the technical bits that happen between your edited final draft and your book being available on bookshelves and online.

But they won't do that first edit for you. They also won't market for you. And this assumes you made it through the slush pile and found a publisher.

I am traditionally published, and if you think you can submit a draft manuscript and walk away to write your next book, you're kidding yourself.

Which brings us to the obvious question why any author would give away all their rights and most of their income to end up doing much of the hard work themselves?

I believe the number one answer to this is because of the perceived cost and difficulty of hiring someone to complete the tasks you either don't have the expertise to complete or don't want to do.

What if I told you there is a way to spend a few hours and a few hundred dollars to offload the tasks you don't want to do or don't possess the technical skills to do?

Most of you would have heard of freelancing and outsourcing. You may also have heard that it's difficult to find competitively-priced freelancers with professional skills, rather than amateurs looking for a quick buck.

This has been the case in the past, but the market has consolidated and matured. The irony is massive layoffs in traditional publishing have contributed to the jump in quality in freelance marketplaces. Many publishing professionals laid off by their employers now make their living as a freelancer.

As an author, there are only two markets you need to consider—Upwork and Reedsy.

Upwork is the 500-pound gorilla in this space; created by the merger of several freelance marketplaces including eLance and RentACoder. Upwork still leans to its IT industry origins and is heavy on programmers and web designers, but it also has an active publishing services marketplace.

Reedsy is a freelance marketplace specializing in publishing services. Launched in 2014, Reedsy's mission is to *"[give] authors and publishers access to talented professionals, powerful tools, and free educational content."*

Comparing the two, Upwork is a bigger marketplace for services other than book publishing, and if you are on a budget, there are more low-priced options on Upwork. The primary advantage of using Reedsy is it's for authors and publishers, so it can be easier to find a professional suited to the job than on Upwork.

If you only want help with publishing and marketing books, I would recommend Reedsy. You will pay more, but you will also get more vetted professionals that specialize in book publishing.

There is a trick to effective use of each platform, which I will show you now.

Using Upwork

1. Search for "upwork", or go to "https://upwork.com" in your favorite browser and sign up for a free account. Once you create your free account on Upwork, your dashboard should look something like the screenshot on the next page.

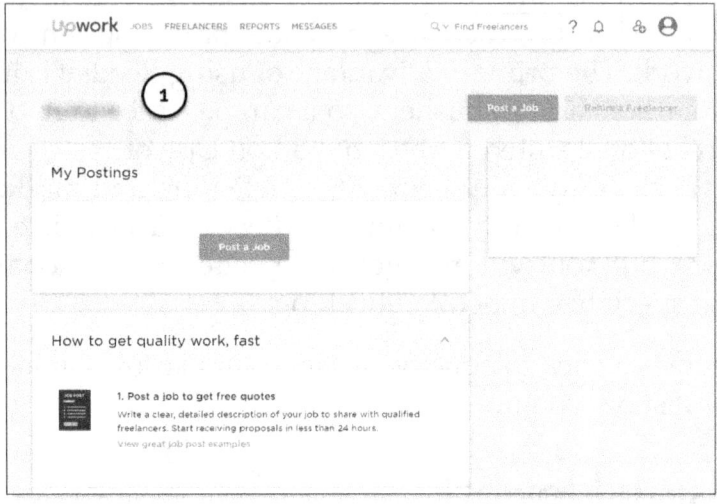

There are two ways to find a freelancer on Upwork:

i. Post a job description so freelancers can submit a quote; or

ii. Find a suitable freelancer and invite them to quote on the job.

Option 1 is useful if you want to feel out the market and review what services are on offer, but I don't recommend it for an efficient long-term option.

Upwork is not selective; anyone can join the platform and offer their services. This means there are thousands of freelancers on Upwork with poor technical skills and even worse English language skills.

If you post an open job, you will most likely need to sift through dozens of opportunistic quotes from low-skilled freelancers to find suitable candidates.

The best way to find a professional on Upwork is to find a freelancer with a good work history and relevant expertise and ask them to provide a quote.

2. Click on "Freelancers" in the top menu and select "Find Freelancers".

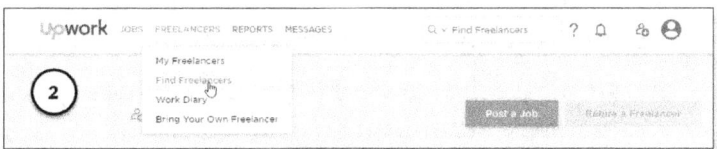

3. Once on the search page, type the job category into the search bar. In this example, I am searching for "editing and proofreading". This search will return thousands of results, so click the **Filters** button.

The filtering options are comprehensive. I find the best results come from the following filter set:

- **Earned Amount—$10K**. You want someone with earnings history.
- **Job Success—90% & up**. The freelancer has completed most of their jobs.
- **Hourly Rate—$10–$30**. You can go higher if you can't find the person you want.
- **Hours Billed—100+ hours**. Similar to Earned Amount, more hours billed means greater experience.
- **Category**. Select a category based on what type of writing you're submitting.
- **English level—Native or bilingual**. Expert or native English is critical for writing-related jobs, but not so much if you want a designer or someone to do a technical job.

The last two filters are not important. As you can see from the screenshot, by the time you filter down to this level, the "Talent Type" and "Last Activity" make little difference to the total number of freelancers in the filtered list.

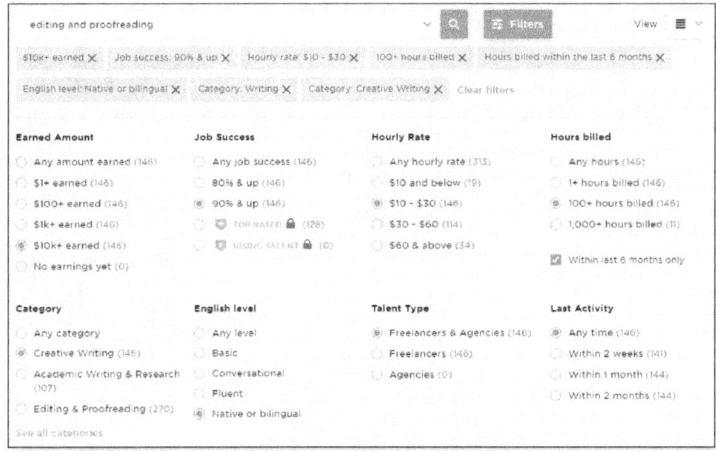

This filter set will give you a list of well-established freelancers with a history of delivering results. Once you apply the filters, you will have a list of between 50 and 150 freelancers. If you are outside this range, tweak the filter.

When you finish filtering, click on the profile link for each candidate, look at their work history, and short-list the ones you like. You need not go through every profile on the list. Once you have short-listed about six candidates, you can stop.

Once you have your short list, open each freelancer's page, and invite them to quote on a job. If you have worked with a freelancer before and want to hire them again, you can also hire them from their profile page.

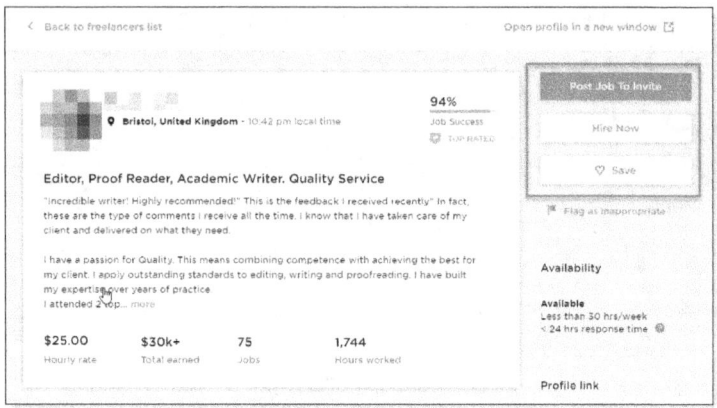

There's not much more to Upwork. Once you and a freelancer agree on the job scope and price, they do the work, and if you're happy, you pay their invoice.

Using Reedsy

Using Reedsy follows a similar process.

4. First, jump over to "https://reedsy.com" and sign up for a free account. Once you sign up, your dashboard should look like the screenshot opposite.

Getting Professional Help

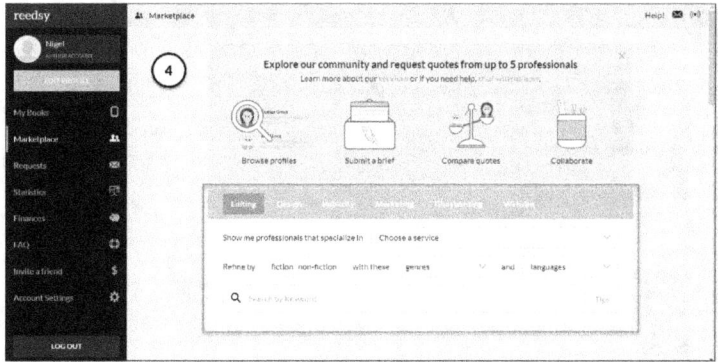

Searching and filtering are much simpler on Reedsy. You can select from Editing, Design, Publicity, Marketing, Ghostwriting and Website categories and filter down by service type, fiction/non-fiction genre, and language.

Once you set the filters, you can explore the filtered list of freelancers for suitable candidates.

What I like about Reedsy is they provide a more detailed list of previous jobs completed by the freelancer than Upwork. This makes it much easier to find someone who has worked on books like yours (screenshot on next page).

This feature is especially useful for finding designers. High-rated designers have portfolio sliders on the search page, and If you open a designer's profile, there's a design gallery. This makes it much easier to find a designer whose style matches your needs.

GETTING PROFESSIONAL HELP 225

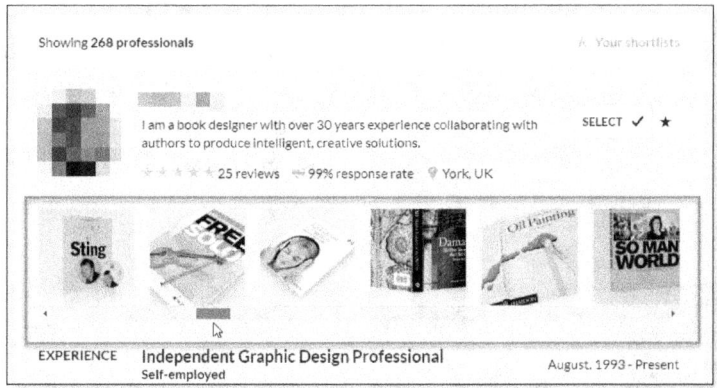

5. Getting quotes on Reedsy is also much easier than Upwork. Click the **Request a Quote** button at the top of the freelancer's profile. You can request a quote from up to 5 different freelancers in the one quote request. Fill out the quote request form and click **Submit Brief** when you're finished.

Take your time to look around both UpWork and Reedsy. Even if you only end up using one or the other, I suggest you sign up for both and see which one you like best.

There is nothing an author will ever need that you won't find on either of these sites. Both services cater to a range of budgets too. You can even hire people to do your marketing and outreach, freeing up even more time for your writing.

And that, dear friends, completes the setup of your very own Indie Publishing Machine. Well done!

You now have an author website, a mailing list to collect email addresses from your fans, and hopefully, some idea how you will conduct outreach to attract more fans.

You also know where to go if you need to hire professional help to build your indie publishing empire.

The last two chapters in the book are for reference.

In the next chapter, I provide answers to common questions about outreach, and in the last chapter, I have collated a list of resources I found helpful in my indie publishing journey.

Chapter 14
Outreach FAQ

As there are hundreds of options for conducting outreach with current and potential fans, it would take an entire book to cover all of them.

In this bonus chapter, I have listed some commentary based on the most common questions I get about self-publishing platforms, social media, marketing, and outreach.

Q: I'm still confused. Is social media good, or bad?

A: Remember the whole point of my approach to book marketing is to find the small number of activities that lead to the biggest results.

Social media is for engagement. It's a 1-on-1 medium by nature, so it performs well for direct communication with fans.

However, social media performs poorly when compared to media like email for promotion, as the vast majority don't see your promotion and those that do either don't care or don't trust you because they don't know you yet.

So:

- Connecting with fans—Social is GOOD
- Drawing potential fans to your website to build trust—Social is GOOD
- Selling books—Social is BAD
- Wasting vast amounts of time when you should be writing—Social is VERY GOOD

Q: So, what's the best outreach strategy for authors?

A: The best outreach strategy depends on where you are in the publishing process:

- **If you don't have a book ready for publication**—write a book. Forget about outreach for now because it will be a waste of your time.
- **If you have a book published**—write another book. Tell your friends, family, writing group, etc. about your book, but do nothing else right now except write a second book. Otherwise, you're wasting your time. If you want to jump right in the deep end—you can publish the book as a series of posts on your website. This is how I got started. This is also how Andy Weir, the author of *The Martian*, got started. It's scary giving away your only book, but it's effective.

- **If you have two books or more published**—read on.

The most effective outreach strategy for authors is also the simplest:

1. You give something you created away in return for an email address; or
2. You publish a piece of content offering a subscription within the content.

Option 1 is much more effective than Option 2 because of the higher perceived value of providing something tangible in return for the reader's email address.

The options are not mutually exclusive. For example, you can publish a post on your website containing a form where the reader can download a PDF version of the post.

You can see this strategy gives you plenty of leeways to experiment with what works for you.

Here are the implementations of this strategy I have found effective:

1. You publish a free book on Amazon with a link to free content on your website that the reader gets in exchange for their email address.
2. You have a popup on your site offering free content in exchange for an email address.
3. Content on your site has sign-up forms embedded in the content.

4. Same as 3, but there is a form in the content offering a free download in return for the reader's email address.
5. You publish free content on your website and link back to it from social groups or guest blog posts.

Remember the basic strategy is what matters, not the specifics. What works for me may not work for you—which is why it's super-important to measure the effectiveness of your outreach.

You also need to remember you are playing the long game here—no single strategy will propel you to the top of the best-seller lists, so aim for strategies you can set and forget so you can continue to build a body of work.

Wattpad

I have a dim view of Wattpad. It's not just the bucket-loads of atrocious teen fiction, but also the fact that Wattpad is cultivating a whole new generation of readers who think everything should be free. Even if I believed you could extract some value from the platform, I avoid it on principle.

Scribd

I must admit I had never heard of Scribd until someone asked my opinion of the service. If you don't know, Scribd is a subscription service for eBooks and audiobooks. It seems to be an improvement on Wattpad in it at least has real books on it (rather than appalling fan fiction), and subscribers must pay. I may put a book on Scribd one day, but I have no advice for you now.

Facebook

I've mentioned Facebook a lot in the book, so I don't have much more to add. Given I practice what I preach, Facebook is the only social media platform I use semi-regularly. I post major news or when I release a book or course. I am in a handful of writing groups where I share some of these updates to increase their reach. I can go weeks without posting anything.

I also maintain a Facebook author page to let Facebook peeps know I am a real person and an author, but I don't post there often.

What this means is, if you want guru advice on how to master Facebook, I'm not the one to ask. I've got this far with my writing career without paying much attention to social media and get much more writing done as a result. If this changes, I will let you know.

Twitter

If you thought the engagement stats were terrible for Facebook, Twitter is worse. The same stats that showed the engagement on Facebook was 0.07%, showed for Twitter it was 0.03%.

Laura Roeder, who is the founder of Meet Edgar, a social media automation platform, did an experiment with her list of over 33,000 followers and found only between 0.6% and 2.5% of her followers saw her tweets and of the few who saw the tweets, only 2% of them clicked the link. The funny thing about this story is her solution to this terrible result was to send more tweets—using Meet Edgar to automate it, of course!

Tim Grahl, whose philosophy is similar to mine, had an author client with 160,000 Twitter followers who used the platform for a book launch. It resulted in less than 400 sales—a 0.02% conversion rate. Another author he worked with had over a million Twitter followers, and a book launch on the platform showed no noticeable difference in book sales.

A commonly cited benefit to Twitter is you can find industry contacts like agents, publishers, and journos on Twitter. As an indie publisher, you don't need an agent or a publisher. Once you build a track record, they will come to you. And journos are everywhere. If you need Twitter to find a journo, you're not looking hard enough.

Twitter is also cited as a great way to meet other authors. I can accept this. Writing is a lonely business, and it is good to build rapport with other authors. But this is not a business decision, it's a social decision and should be conducted during downtime, not work time.

Instagram and Pinterest

I've never opened an account on either platform, nor used them, so I have no advice for you. Refer to my previous comments on practicing what I preach—Facebook is my primary social channel, and I don't touch the others. If I ever add to my 20% and open an Instagram or Pinterest account, I will let you know how it goes.

Social Automation

Social automation is where you pay a monthly fee to companies like Hootsuite or Meet Edgar for the convenience of scheduling social media posts, so you don't have to do it by hand.

If you plan on joining the "post until your fingers bleed" cult, this can save you time. Otherwise, you're just wasting your money.

Author Blog

An author blog is valid for two use cases:

1. Non-fiction authors should post articles and

book excerpts in their area of expertise. This is good for building credibility with readers, provides a quality target for outreach, and is excellent for search engine ranking as readers link and share your content.

2. Fiction authors should post short stories, book excerpts, world-building, and backstory content. The reasons are the same as for non-fiction, except the intent is to draw readers into your worlds, not to build credibility.

Unless you are a compulsive sharer, all other forms of blog content are low-value and unnecessary for your success. If you *are* a compulsive sharer, make your blog your go-to place for posting and link back from social, rather than post to social first, as this is an easy way to turn a time-waster into a valuable bit of outreach.

Other Blogs

Posting to other blogs (guest blogging) is outreach. You need to prepare your 5Ws and monitor to see if the result was worth the effort.

Book Launches

The book launch is a carryover from the old days of traditional publishing where a publisher needed to move a crap-ton of copies to recoup their costs.

Big book launches are not only unnecessary for an indie but don't often return a benefit that outweighs the time, cost, and stress of trying to coordinate the launch.

I do what I call a low-key launch that is 20% effort, 80% results. I could put more effort in and push up the results, but I find it's not worth the stress for an extra few sales.

My launch process:

1. **Email your list** saying you will publish a new book soon. Have a link in the email they can click to register their interest.
2. **Publish the book**. Publishing on Amazon is never a smooth process, so it's best to make sure the book is published and available on Amazon. This will save you massive amounts of stress, trust me. Don't worry about the book being available before the official launch. Unless you are a big-name author, your book will be invisible on Amazon until you have made quite a few sales.
3. **Send another email to your list** outlining your "official" launch—where the book will be available for a launch price of $0.99 (the lowest you can set it to on Amazon) for a few days only (7 days max). Ask them to click a link if they want to agree to leave you a review.
4. **The day before the official launch, set the price to $0.99 on Amazon and then send another email** saying that the launch starts tomorrow.

Link to the book page on Amazon in this email. Don't try to synchronize the price drop with your email. Amazon takes a few hours to update pricing, and your readers will be in many time zones, so it's pointless trying.

5. **Send an email on launch day.** Link to the book page on Amazon. Repeat the request for reviewers.
6. **Send an email the day before the launch ends.** Link to the book page on Amazon. Ask if they bought the book. Include a link to the review page so those who purchased the book can leave a review.
7. **A week after launch, email all review volunteers** asking them if they left a review. Include a link to the book review page for those who haven't left a review yet.
8. **Send an email a month after the launch ends.** Link to the book page on Amazon. Ask if they bought the book. Include a link to the review page so those who purchased the book can leave a review.

The cool thing about this process is it's automatic. I write the sequence once in my email program and copy and change the sequence for each book launch. It took a few hours to get the sequence right the first time, and about an hour to update the links and test for each new book. Then I forget about it.

You can use the same sequence with minimal modification to run a special on the same book every few months. From experience, the specials are just as effective as the original launch in generating new sales and new reviews.

Ads

Advertising is unnecessary for your success and is not a part of the 20% effort that will get you 80% of your results. Once you are established, however, they can be worth considering. Social media ads can be an excellent way to draw people to your work because you can get quite granular with your targeting.

The downside is it's easy to lose money if you aren't careful. Ads are high-risk for a new author as "buy my book" advertising doesn't work. To get a conversion rate that doesn't contain a lot of zeroes, your ads must point to free content. This free content must contain a Call to Action (CTA) to paid content.

When an Internet user sees an ad, their trust goes down. To get them to follow through to a paid option, you need to regain their trust, which means you must offer something of value at no cost. My advice: get great at your organic marketing before you consider advertising.

Permafree

Permafree is where you list your book on Amazon with the price set to zero. You can't set your book price to zero in KDP as Amazon has a minimum price of $0.99. You first must list your book on a site where you can set the price to free (e.g., Barnes and Noble) and then email Amazon to get them to price match.

I rate permafree second only to free downloads on your author website for building an audience. It's not as valuable as it once was because so many free books are published on Amazon, but you can still expect 5-10 times as many downloads for a free book as a paid book—even if the reader is only paying 99 cents. As long as your book has quality CTA's inside, permafree is still a good way to increase your fan-base.

Kindle Select

I can't offer any specific advice—I sell books on my author website, so don't qualify for Kindle Select. I suggest an effective strategy could be using free days with the same sequence I outlined in the section on "Book Launches".

Chapter 15
Resources

A list of references from the book plus additional books, websites and other resources that I have found invaluable on my own writers journey.

Websites

Author Earnings. This site has been closed down, but you can still find the reports and articles in the Internet Archive.

https://web.archive.org/web/*/http://authorearnings.com/

Book Map. 2017 Global eBook market report.

https://www.wischenbart.com/page-59

Author's Guild of America. report

https://www.authorsguild.org/industry-advocacy/authors-guild-survey-shows-drastic-42-percent-decline-in-authors-earnings-in-last-decade/

Book Launch. This is Tim Grahl's website (author of *Your First 1000 Copies*). Some great articles and free tips. Social *vs.* Email stats are quoted in this article:

https://booklaunch.com/social-media-marketing-authors/

The Creative Penn. Author resources site created by Joanna Penn. Has some great free and paid content, although Joanna falls into the "post until your fingers bleed" camp, so use your own judgement.

https://www.thecreativepenn.com/

Thrive Themes. Don't let the WordPress theme site bit fool you - Thrive is not only the best WordPress theme available for authors (I use them on all my sites), but their blog and Thrive University is worth the price of the subscription just for the goldmine of content marketing advice and resources they have on their site. I advise all authors looking beyond the basics of WordPress themes and marketing check them out.

https://thrivethemes.com/.

Placeit. Phone and computer mockups.

https://placeit.net/

PSD Covers. Book mockups (requires Photoshop).

https://www.psdcovers.com/

Prolific Works. Book marketing and promotion.

https://www.prolificworks.com/authors

Freebooksy. Book marketing and promotion.

https://www.freebooksy.com/for-the-authors/

Hidden Gems Books. Service for providing Advance Reader Copies (ARCs) to readers.

https://www.hiddengemsbooks.com/

Reedsy Discovery. Book marketing and promotion.

https://reedsy.com/discovery

Alliance of Independent Authors (ALLi). ALLi have a huge library of resources for self-publishing authors, including guide books, articles and a range of support services for members.

https://www.allianceindependentauthors.org/

Copy Blogger. If you want you outreach to be effective, it needs to adhere to good copywriting principles. There are hundreds of online resources for improving your copywriting skills, but Copy Blogger is my favorite. Membership is free.

https://my.copyblogger.com/

Bowker Identifier Services. You should never accept free ISBNs from any publisher, as they will be listed as the publisher of the book. Bowker is the international broker for ISBNs. You can also buy barcodes for your ISBNs.

https://www.myidentifiers.com/

Books

A list of books I found helpful in my indie publishing journey. I have dozens more books on writing craft, but have only include the ones that help the publishing side of your business, for example, creating well-structured story outlines so you can write books faster and reduce editing time.

Authority by Nathan Barry

The E-Myth by Michael E. Gerber

The 7 Habits of Highly Effective People by Stephen R. Covey

Deep Work by Cal Newport

Save the Cat! Writes a Novel by Jessica Brody

Grit: The Power of Passion by Angela Duckworth

Write. Publish. Repeat by Sean Platt and Johnny B. Truant

Discoverability by Kristine Kathryn Rusch

Essentialism by Greg McKeown

Marketing for Writers Who Hate Marketing by James Scott Bell

How to Write Short Stories and Use Them to Further Your Writing Career by James Scott Bell

The Story Grid by Shawn Coyne

Nobody Wants to Read Your Sh*t by Steven Pressfield

Revision and Self-Editing for Publication by James Scott Bell

Your First 1000 Copies by Tim Grahl

The War of Art by Steven Pressfield

Hustle by Neil Patel, Patrick Vlaskovits and Jonas Koffler

How to Get Things Done by David Allen

Reinventing You by Dorie Clark

Stand Out by Dorie Clark

Wired for Story Lisa Cron

Outliers: The Story of Success by Malcolm Gladwell

The One Thing by Gary Keller

Writing Fiction for All You're Worth James Scott Bell

2K to 10K: Writing Faster by Rachel Aaron

1500 Words Per Hour by N.P. Martin

How to Make a Living as a Writer by James Scott Bell

Marketing Without Money by Tom Patty

www.ingramcontent.com/pod-product-compliance
Lightning Source LLC
Chambersburg PA
CBHW070542010526
44118CB00012B/1193